Democracy: A Very Short Introduction

VERY SHORT INTRODUCTIONS are for anyone wanting a stimulating and accessible way into a new subject. They are written by experts, and have been translated into more than 45 different languages.

The series began in 1995, and now covers a wide variety of topics in every discipline. The VSI library currently contains over 700 volumes—a Very Short Introduction to everything from Psychology and Philosophy of Science to American History and Relativity—and continues to grow in every subject area.

Very Short Introductions available now:

ABOLITIONISM Richard S. Newman
THE ABRAHAMIC RELIGIONS
    Charles L. Cohen
ACCOUNTING Christopher Nobes
ADDICTION Keith Humphreys
ADOLESCENCE Peter K. Smith
THEODOR W. ADORNO
    Andrew Bowie
ADVERTISING Winston Fletcher
AERIAL WARFARE Frank Ledwidge
AESTHETICS Bence Nanay
AFRICAN AMERICAN HISTORY
    Jonathan Scott Holloway
AFRICAN AMERICAN RELIGION
    Eddie S. Glaude Jr
AFRICAN HISTORY John Parker and
    Richard Rathbone
AFRICAN POLITICS Ian Taylor
AFRICAN RELIGIONS
    Jacob K. Olupona
AGEING Nancy A. Pachana
AGNOSTICISM Robin Le Poidevin
AGRICULTURE Paul Brassley and
    Richard Soffe
ALEXANDER THE GREAT
    Hugh Bowden
ALGEBRA Peter M. Higgins
AMERICAN BUSINESS HISTORY
    Walter A. Friedman
AMERICAN CULTURAL HISTORY
    Eric Avila
AMERICAN FOREIGN RELATIONS
    Andrew Preston
AMERICAN HISTORY Paul S. Boyer

AMERICAN IMMIGRATION
    David A. Gerber
AMERICAN INTELLECTUAL
    HISTORY
    Jennifer Ratner-Rosenhagen
THE AMERICAN JUDICIAL SYSTEM
    Charles L. Zelden
AMERICAN LEGAL HISTORY
    G. Edward White
AMERICAN MILITARY HISTORY
    Joseph T. Glatthaar
AMERICAN NAVAL HISTORY
    Craig L. Symonds
AMERICAN POETRY David Caplan
AMERICAN POLITICAL HISTORY
    Donald Critchlow
AMERICAN POLITICAL PARTIES
    AND ELECTIONS L. Sandy Maisel
AMERICAN POLITICS
    Richard M. Valelly
THE AMERICAN PRESIDENCY
    Charles O. Jones
THE AMERICAN REVOLUTION
    Robert J. Allison
AMERICAN SLAVERY
    Heather Andrea Williams
THE AMERICAN SOUTH
    Charles Reagan Wilson
THE AMERICAN WEST
    Stephen Aron
AMERICAN WOMEN'S HISTORY
    Susan Ware
AMPHIBIANS T. S. Kemp
ANAESTHESIA Aidan O'Donnell

For more information visit our website

www.oup.com/vsi/

Naomi Zack

DEMOCRACY

A Very Short Introduction

Great Clarendon Street, Oxford, OX2 6DP,
United Kingdom

Oxford University Press is a department of the University of Oxford.
It furthers the University's objective of excellence in research, scholarship,
and education by publishing worldwide. Oxford is a registered trade mark of
Oxford University Press in the UK and in certain other countries

Published in the United States of America by Oxford University Press
198 Madison Avenue, New York, NY 10016, United States of America

British Library Cataloguing in Publication Data
Data available

Library of Congress Control Number: 2022951440

ISBN 978-0-19-284506-1

Printed by Integrated Books International, United States of America

To my granddaughters, Cloe and Winona, may democracy continue to get better in your time

Contents

Acknowledgments

The text for this VSI was written and revised over a two-year period. I am very grateful to my students at Lehman College, CUNY, for their feedback on early versions of the manuscript as I taught different iterations of a course called "Democracy: Intellectual and Historical Developments." Imogene Haslam, as Project Editor, has provided expert coordination through production. Thanks also to Production Management Executive Ethiraju Saraswathi of Straive.com, for overseeing production. My greatest debt for the coherence and readability of the book is to Dr. Latha Menon, Senior Commissioning Editor for the VSI Series. Latha provideded invaluable support through revisions of both the initial proposal and the completed manuscript. Her advice and editing were extraordinarily conscientious and incisive, and I thank her for the existence of the book.

Naomi Zack

Bronx, NY
March 3, 2023

List of illustrations

Chapter 1
Thinking about democracy: tools for understanding

People who live in democracies, especially rich democracies, are generally safe and comfortable. They have opportunities for self-advancement and are optimistic about the future. More people attempt to immigrate than are admitted. That is the ideal, and the benefits of democracy are easily taken for granted by those who have them. Others, who are poor, non-white, non-male, disabled, non-heterosexual, or non-binary cannot take the ideal as reality. They aspire to or demand the benefits of democracy and, what is very important, believe that democracy itself allows for them to attain its benefits.

Complacency about democracy, for both those who have its benefits and those who strive for them, was jolted during President Trump's administration in the United States. On January 6, 2021, after Trump had lost the 2020 election and called it "stolen," his supporters stormed the US capitol, with some chanting "Hang Mike Pence," the Vice-President, whose job it was to preside over the Senate certification of the 2020 election (Figure 1). This violent uprising was quelled, hundreds were criminally charged and sentenced, and congressional investigation followed. But many conservatives, progressives, activists, and legal scholars believe that American democracy is "in peril." They are reacting to both the eruption of violence and disorder on January 6,

1. "Trump Supporters Hold 'Stop The Steal' Rally In DC Amid Ratification Of Presidential Election."

and its intent to disrupt normal democratic procedures for the peaceful transition of government after a democratic election.

Such dangers to democratic procedures are not limited to American politics. Internationally, threats to democracy can be existential. Russian military aggression against Ukraine in early 2022 breached the security of a democratic sovereign nation. If a democratic sovereign nation is taken over by an undemocratic one, internal democracy will collapse. Internal democracy may also be threatened by elected officials with authoritarian ties and leanings. When French President Emmanuel Macron handily won re-election against right-wing populist candidate Marine LePen in April 2022 (58.5 percent to 41.5 percent), the democratic world of NATO and the US heartily congratulated him and breathed a sigh of relief.

Both internal and external threats to democracy make it urgent to think systematically about what democracy is and how it came about, so that it can be protected. From a philosophical-historical perspective, that is the purpose of this book. What is democracy? What it means now is different from what it meant in the ancient world or the 18th century. Even today, not all that is called "democracy" resembles what people who live in real democracies mean by the word. Still, some past meanings of "democracy" that would not qualify as "democracy" now contributed to our present ideals and realities of democracy. We can start with several general definitions: Democracies are nations containing both governments and their societies that are democratic; Democracy is an ideal for the best form of government and its related society; Democracies are democratic practices and institutions in both government and society. The word "democracy" thus refers to actual nations and societies, forms of government, and political practices. But what makes them democratic?

The Pew Research Center refers to 2017 sources that ranked the 195 countries in the world according to how democratic they are, based on: electoral process and pluralism, civil liberties, the functioning of government, political participation, and political culture. Specific factors are considered to be very important: freeness and fairness of national elections, security of voters, protection against foreign-power influence, and the capability of civil servants to implement policies. The quality of political life is also important. According to all these measures, although about half of all the world's countries can be considered democracies, only 22 are "full" democracies. Pew ranked them in order: Norway, Iceland, Sweden, New Zealand, Finland, Ireland, Denmark, Canada, Australia, Switzerland, Netherlands, Luxembourg, Germany, United Kingdom, Uruguay, Austria, Spain, Mauritius, Costa Rica, France, Chile, Portugal. Another 46 countries, including the United States, were assessed as "flawed" democracies. Of course, any such ranking is subject to criticism of the standards used and how they have been applied and computed. But the overall project tells us how expert observers now view democracies.

In this *Very Short Introduction* to democracy, I will begin by providing a descriptive philosophical distinction considering different instances of democracy and uses of the word. This is the distinction between the *concept* of democracy and *conceptions* of democracy. It is like the distinction between fruit and apples or pears, or between dogs and poodles and basset hounds. Not everyone will welcome this distinction, so I will also discuss normative ideals of democracy that claim to express what democracy really is. Statements of such ideals are normative, because they imply that actors in the real world should strive for them. The second section is about actual democracies and forms of democratic government, and the third section is a consideration of traditional and alternative historical approaches to democracy. Finally, I offer a brief discussion of my methodology in the book, together with an overview of Chapters 2–8.

Conceptual and normative approaches

As a philosopher, I prefer to view democracy as a *concept* that almost everyone can *grasp*. A concept is an idea that is the shared meaning of a word. Because it can be widely shared, the concept of democracy is abstract and general. As *abstract*, the concept does not refer to anything in reality—it is a thought. As *general*, the concept of democracy is also vague, but it can refer to all of its concrete instances that specify it in ways that are meant to describe conditions in the world, and it also refers to all of its *conceptions*. A conception of democracy is a description of a particular meaning of the abstract concept. A conception of democracy is more particular than the abstract general concept. For instance, we can say of the concept of democracy that it vaguely and generally means that those who are governed have a say in that government. A conception of democracy might specify universal suffrage so that all adult citizens can vote. A competing conception of democracy may specify that only those adults who are educated or own property can vote. Conceptions of democracy change over time and place. Our present best conception of democracy may include universal recognition of human rights. That is a relatively new conception, dating from the 1948 United Nations Universal Declaration of Human Rights (see Appendix). Older conceptions of democracy excluded certain humans from rights recognition. And future conceptions of democracy may extend the recognition of rights to non-human life forms.

However, there is no guarantee that future conceptions of democracy will continue to be more inclusive, or "better." And there may also be arguably (contested or competing) best conceptions of democracy in the present. Whether reasoning over past, present, and future, or considering competing or contested conceptions of democracy in the present, it is important to emphasize that there is nothing relative about such competing conceptions, because arguments need to be made for which is the best conception at any given time.

The word "democracy" refers to a mental "something" that is its concept—a concept is the meaning of a word—and this concept need not refer to any actual thing outside of people's minds. The concept of democracy is, again, vaguely, a kind of government in which those governed have influence over that government. Governments have been called "democratic" if they have a division of powers, elections are free, the majority can make decisions for everyone, the rights of individuals are respected by the government, those governed are treated equally, there is a free press and free dissent, and those governed generally consent to their existing government but retain a right to change it. None of these traits of democratic government define "democracy," because not everyone who uses the word means all or most of them, or even perhaps any of them. But as a general, shared concept, democracy vaguely refers to a form of government in which those governed consent to their government and are able and allowed to participate in it. But this is still not a fully adequate definition because a vague concept cannot be defined. However, a concept can be specified through its conceptions.

The democratic traits already mentioned and others that are associated with the concept of democracy have been and can continue to be combined, fleshed out, and applied, according to different *conceptions* of democracy. Conceptions of democracy specify it in a particular time and place—conceptions of democracy depend on their contexts. Past conceptions of democracy may include or leave out factors important to our modern conceptions of democracy. For example, from the ancient world until well into the 19th century, the leading conception of democracy permitted slavery, but no one today would include slavery in their conception of democracy.

The word "democracy" thus refers to both an abstract concept and its more concrete conceptions. Real nations with democratic governments are also called "democracies." Democracies usually include, in founding documents or traditional practices (or both), rule by law and practices that uphold political freedoms. The leading conception of democracy in the early 21st century is an ideal of morally good government. Past conceptions of democracy have varied from (negative) descriptions of mob rule in the ancient world, to advocacy of rights for middle-class white men in the modern period, to Marxist ideas of the ascendancy of the working class. Through both affirmation and criticism, these past conceptions have led to present progressive conceptions that center justice and equality for all, including racial and ethnic minorities, women, LGBTQ+(?) people, the poor, indigenous people, disabled people, and other disadvantaged human groups.

Conceptions of democracy need not be explicit, because a group may suddenly arise to demand democratic treatment that was previously denied, without naming the conception of democracy that it is invoking. Still, a theorist may be able to infer implicit or inchoate conceptions. For instance, demands for greater government protection against gun violence rely on a conception of democratic government as a central authority that keeps the peace. Gun owners and manufacturers may lobby against government regulation of gun ownership and sales, based on a conception of democracy that holds individual liberty sacrosanct.

The concept of democracy thus supports multiple conceptions. This variety in conception does not mean that differences are merely semantic. Rather, different conceptions of democracy are associated with different concrete past and present circumstances. And they may describe existing democratic governments. For example, after the Civil War, US conceptions of democracy excluded slavery, whereas before the Civil War, slavery was included. Approaching specific ideas about democracy as conceptions of the general concept allows us to recognize ideas about democracy that we may not accept now. This is not relativism, because it can be shown that some conceptions of democracy are more democratic than others. For instance, a conception of democracy that excludes slavery is more democratic than one which includes it.

Conceptions of democracy are not "just ideas," because they are related to real governments and institutions. If a conception of democracy is aspirational—and not only descriptive—it should be possible to explain how it can come about, that is, what existing government structures or social institutions it builds on or could innovate. For example, women's suffrage was included in 19th-century conceptions of democracy, before women were allowed to vote; the absence of legal slavery was part of a conception of democracy before slavery was outlawed. In both cases, it was possible and ultimately practical to describe democracy without exclusively male suffrage or slavery. A conception of democracy in which animals have rights or stronger environmental preservation is legally protected would require recognition of animal-rights human advocacy or the need to expand existing environmental protection legislation.

Aspirational conceptions of democracy have histories in political movements, as well as changes toward greater inclusion within governments that are already democratic. Political aspiration can inspire individuals and move multitudes to demand government change, through rhetoric, scholarly treatises, and popular demonstration and protest. For instance, the 2011 Occupy Movement in the United States raised international awareness of unprecedented inequalities in wealth and income, as support and protests spread to 951 cities in 82 countries. But this awareness did not quickly result in legal changes to economic inequalities.

Leading conceptions of democracy change over time. During the second half of the 20th century until the present, both progressive activist movements and scholarly work have been motivated by a democratic conception of social equality. Activists and academics in the humanities and social sciences have often been the avant-garde of new, egalitarian conceptions of democracy. Activists have protested undemocratic or unjust treatment of members of disadvantaged groups in society, such as women, LGBTQ+(?) groups, people of color, and disabled people. Academics have sought to analyze, ameliorate, and improve the conditions of these groups by forging new subfields across existing disciplines, such as feminism, critical race theory, philosophy of race, and post-colonial studies. There have also been innovations in scholarly methods: standpoint theory aims to give voice to those excluded or powerless, by speaking from their circumstances; intersectionality focuses on those who experience multiple oppressions. Both new subfields in existing disciplines and methodological innovations, together with activism based on them, may ultimately motivate new conceptions of democracy.

Not everyone would be receptive to the philosophical concept–conception distinction of meanings of "democracy" that I am proposing. One reason is that it sounds relative, as though all conceptions are equally good. Some begin with what they think democracy *really is*, as an ideal that does or does not exist in reality. A contrast between that ideal can be made with what is called "democracy" that falls short of the ideal, with the implication that what falls short of the ideal *should* be brought up to it. The "should" makes this comparison a normative approach. Defining democracy in this normative way allows for the identification of democratic failure at a given time (as in the rankings described earlier) or misnomer. For instance, when a nation with an authoritarian government calls itself a democracy, those with a contemporary normative ideal of democracy can say that nation is not a democracy. But, as noted, arguments can also be provided in favor of a particular conception of democracy. (In this case, comparison of what is called "democracy" between authoritarian and non-authoritarian conceptions.) So the difference between a concept–conception approach and a contextualized normative approach may not amount to much.

However, direct normative approaches to democracy do seek moral justification, with a number of plausible reasons that point to benefits for those democratically governed: Democracy allows for the interests of those governed to be furthered through their political participation; Democratic government functions better; Democratic decision making draws on broad intellectual resources; Democracy supports individual liberty and autonomy, which are intrinsic human goods, and at the same time, there is public (transparent) decision making that treats people as equals, in the parts of their lives shared under government. These are moral issues because they pertain to human well-being. But, moral reasons can also be given in favor of or against different conceptions of democracy. Sometimes, the morally bad nature of a conception of democracy, for instance one that approves slavery, is self-evident. But other times, moral value may be debatable, for instance in discussion about the compatibility of capitalism with democracy. Throughout this book, I will find the concept–conception distinction for ideas of democracy useful, together with the implied understanding that not all conceptions of democracy are morally or ethically equal.

Factors of democracy

Governments are ruling institutions in society that perform functions, such as taxation and defense, which less powerful parts of society cannot do on their own. Governments also have ultimate physical power or force, within their societies. Historically, democracies have been actual national governments that express their norms of government in founding documents, laws, and/or traditional practices. Democratic governments are distinguished by their histories and the cultures within societies associated with them. After the Treaty of Westphalia in 1648, the traditional unit of democracy has been the nation state, as a geographically bounded sovereign entity. Democracies are nations with democratic governments.

Many accounts of the founding and origins of democratic nation states feature relief from cruel and unjust tyranny and exploitive oppression. Democratic governmental structures were also designed to restrain human greed for wealth and power, although only among elites until the 20th century. With free speech, democracies allow for ongoing criticism and disagreement about these restraints. For example, objection to inequalities of wealth and income by those who have less may be countered by the inertia of such inequality or even efforts to increase it. This process of disagreement has no natural equilibrium and democracies are not set up to achieve that. Still, in general, several conceptual tools are useful for understanding how democracy and democracies work: inclusion; participatory or direct versus representative government; divisions of government powers; federalism.

Inclusion and participation. Two major questions have structured both actual democratic governments and conceptions of them: Who are the people who will have a say in governing? This is the question of inclusion. Should democratic government be direct or representative? This is the question of participation. The question of inclusion involves the voting and participation rights of citizens, which were first restricted to adult male property owners. It can be answered historically through descriptions of the expansion of suffrage to include poor men, women, and members of racial and ethnic minority groups. The second question is related to the first in terms of the formal structure of government, and in the modern period it has largely been answered in favor of representative over direct democracy: The people—however they are designated at a given time—democratically elect their representatives, who will carry out the functions of government.

Direct or participatory democracy allows for those governed to directly make government decisions. In otherwise representative governments, popular referenda may sometimes be held and that is another instance of direct democracy. Examples of recent referenda include the United Kingdom's decision to leave the European Union in 2016 and the US State of California's rejection of Affirmative Action in 2020. Direct democracy sounds as though it is more democratic than representative democracy and it is if the electorate is small enough so that all members can participate. But there can be direct democracy with only an elite part of the population allowed to participate, as in ancient Greece, and there can be representative government with universal adult suffrage, as in modern democracies.

Broad universal adult suffrage can also be restricted by gerrymandering or politically drawing the boundaries of electoral districts so that members of specific groups do not have sufficient majorities to carry a district. Voter suppression may outright bar racial or ethnic minorities from polling places or create obstacles to voting that mainly apply to them. Gerrymandering and voter suppression involve both inclusion and participation.

Over the modern period, disputes about changes within what are considered the most democratic governments have been about who should be permitted to have a say in government, that is, who should be included within participants. After the American Revolutionary period, there was ardent disagreement about whether the new country should be set up as a democracy or a republic, which roughly meant direct versus representative democracy. It was then assumed and approved that representative government would filter out uninformed voters. By the 19th century, fears of universal suffrage were expressed as fear of how working-class people could be manipulated by the rich and well educated. In *The English Constitution* (1867), Walter Bagehot called this a change of *vox populi* into *vox diaboli*. Such concern about an under-educated electorate carries into present worries about the circulation of conspiracy theories and the spread of conservative white-supremacist and xenophobic populism.

The distinction between democracies and republics has further importance if democracies are simply governed by majority rule, in contrast to governments in republics that can safeguard the rights of [numerical] minorities when the majority votes to infringe them. Benjamin Franklin's remark, "It's a republic, if you can keep it," referred to apprehensions among US founders of the winner-takes-all dangers of party politics. Democracy was suspect, because the majority was believed to be uninformed or biased against elite minorities—the majority might be unjust after gaining power.

Divisions within government. Conceptions of democratic governments have emphasized rule by law that provides for both divisions within central government powers and sub-national government structures. Constitutions specifying basic citizen rights, general principles of government, and the structure of government may be written out, as in the United States, or based on well-established legal traditions, as in the United Kingdom. Democratic division of government is in accord with the doctrine attributed to Charles de Secondat, Baron de Montesquieu's *The Spirit of Law* published in 1748. Montesquieu's main idea was that those who make the laws, the legislature, have power and authority distinct from the executive, who heads the government and applies the laws; an independent judiciary is a third power capable of checking both the executive and legislature.

Federalism. Not all democracies consist of simply one government with authority over those governed. Federalism is a government structure that divides power between a national, central government, and smaller, usually geographical units, such as states. Some federal systems, as in Canada, assign more power to the national government; others to states, as in the United States, although central and state powers and authority frequently overlap. Overall, the authority of the national government and its constitution usually pre-empt the authority of state governments and their constitutions. The division of government power can be quite complicated, so that government power is shared beyond the broad divisions in federal systems. State governments within the United States may share their powers with more local government units such as counties, cities, boroughs, and townships. Many different arrangements are possible and different interests require open negotiations and a general sense of commonality and cooperation in order to avoid constitutional crises, civil war, gridlock, or towns where neighbors hate one another.

Power divisions in federal systems can have real teeth. In the United States, during the COVID-19 pandemic, politically Democratic states imposed stricter mitigation measures than Republican states. This difference was possible because US states have jurisdiction over public health. Before the 2022 mid-term election, Republican state legislatures passed voter restriction rules that are believed to be obstacles to minority voting. Such political party differences can become ad hoc government structures that further or undermine ideals of democracy. Both federalism and partisan politics show that we should not assume that democratic nation states are thoroughly unified by a national government. Rather, the differences and disagreements among and within state and local governments amount to a democratic structure among more local governments—excluding civil war.

Democracy is not limited to forms of government within nation states. There are also relations among nations, and institutions within societies connected to respective governments. Global democratic relations among nations remain aspirational in the early 21st century. Superpowers dominate throughout the world, sometimes in unstable détente, and there are extreme gaps in rights and human well-being among nations. Diplomatic processes have resulted in international agreements such as trade treaties, cooperative regulative projects, and military alliances. Diplomatic negotiations are also constant. In addition, democratic nations may newly emerge.

Overall, sovereignty is the most important characteristic of democratic nations or divisions within them. Sovereignty entails a freedom to act among other political units. The individual's counterpart to sovereignty is autonomy, a liberty to do anything that the law does not forbid. (The double negative is necessary here, because usually only what is unlawful is explicitly defined.)

Historical approaches to democracy

World Western dominance has been reflected in dominant Western conceptions of democracy. Since the 17th century, Westerners have assumed that democracy was reinvented in the Euro-American tradition, in direct descent from democracy in ancient Greece and Rome. Thus, leading historical accounts often begin with ancient Greece and Rome and then go straight to the Magna Carta, the American Revolution, and the French Revolution. As a result, non-Western democratic practices in Asia, Africa, the Middle East, and among indigenous groups—albeit some of them in institutions and regions within nations—have not received robust scholarly attention. Also, historical accounts often omit consideration of democratic institutions and practices in medieval Europe.

Nobel laureate Amartya Sen has attributed part of this neglect to a Western emphasis on voting, compared to free public discourse. Sen believes that Eurocentric racism also contributes to such omissions. Many of the overlooked historical democratic practices emphasized free public discussion and criticism or *public reason*, without broad electoral practices.

In considering intellectual and historical conceptions of democracy, it is vital to recognize the inherently disruptive effects of new conceptions of democracy and changes into democratic government. New democratic arrangements instituted by government are likely to contradict existing status rankings and well-established hierarchies of privilege in society. Philosopher Jacques Rancière argues in his 2007 *Hatred of Democracy* that the spontaneity of democratic demands means that democracy is "government of anybody and everybody." Rancière claims that as a result, those with rank and status who are already in power in both society and government hate democracy.

Those seeking to expand democracy within a nation state or make it more inclusive are usually motivated by conceptions of justice. The concept of justice, like the concept of democracy, is vaguely, but universally grasped. The concept of justice is more abstract and general than the concept of democracy and some conceptions of democracy may seem unjust in comparison to others. Many could not say what their conception of justice is. Instead, injustice is more easily and likely to be identified. Protests and demonstrations may suddenly erupt against an immediate outrage, to be accompanied with chants of "No Justice, No Peace." The concept of justice, which includes people getting what they morally deserve, according to decisions made by government officials, only vaguely connotes a kind of order or the restoration of order in society under government.

In this VSI, I aim to combine historical contexts with key ideas or themes that are relevant to present democratic realities and ideals. The themes of what we—people of good will, humanitarians, progressives, political scholars—now consider to be democracy or democratic can be related to past ideas in their historical contexts. Sometimes thinkers have directly influenced political events and other times they have been influenced by them. Overall, influence may be a slow process, with insights of one century not coming to fruition in reality until the next century, or even later. The relationship between history and ideas is complicated and even mysterious. But it seems natural to study them together, ideas in their historical contexts and political periods with their accompanying ideas. Ideas and realities in their times go together. However, I am not providing historical narratives to connect historical events, but rather to contextualize historical thought about democracy. The result should be a historically contextualized story of conceptions of democracy from the ancient world to the present—from a philosophical perspective. In retrospect, this story suggests connections between ideas and events, or at least our ability to say, "If not for X, Y would have been very different." For instance, without social contract theory, the American and French revolutions would have had different justifications. And without the moral reform perspectives of Rousseau, Bentham, Mill, and Marx, ideas and movements toward democracy in society, outside of government, might not have occurred when they did. By the same token, it does not require a philosopher to point out the cumulative effects of democratic institutions over time. For instance, democratic deliberative bodies throughout the world supported the development of democratic structures in modern nation states.

Over the following chapters, democracy in the ancient world (Chapter 2) is followed by democratic structures in the medieval and Renaissance period (Chapter 3). The social contract is then explored as the theme of early modern statecraft (Chapter 4). Rights became important goals during the American and French revolutions (Chapter 5). Nineteenth-century moral progressivism was an important shift in focus from democratic government to democratic society (Chapter 6). The period of World War II influenced much of 20th-century thought about democracy, as well as new forms of activism (Chapter 7). Finally, although we can consider only history and current events, we do know the shape of current threats to democracy. Problems such as climate change, pandemics, and undemocratic populism will likely need to be addressed in the future (Chapter 8).

The general subject of democracy is more complicated from a philosophical perspective than a first approach might reveal. As a result, analysis might seem too dry for the spirit of democracy and its almost universal appeal. But it is my hope that the trajectory of the book will kindle political optimism in readers. Democracy, even when people falsely believe that something is democratic when it is not, has a distinctive spirit. The descendants of people who are passionate about preserving what they consider democracy now may look back and shake their heads. But they will do so because they think that what they consider democracy to be much better, much more democratic. And we hope they will be right.

Chapter 2
Democracy in the ancient world: Greece, Rome, and beyond

Some historians have speculated that before recorded history and the institution of government, hunter-gatherer groups were democratic, because they shared work and property. Survival of all would have required cooperation and even altruism. Decisions may have been made by vote or acclaim. There is no path from unrecorded to recorded history, but such speculation gets us thinking about democracy in units smaller than nations. Indeed, recorded history provides evidence of democracy in much smaller political units than nations, which have supported democracy in larger units that encompass them or learn from them. We also know that democracy can spread.

We imagine democracy coming from the people who want a say in government. Ironically, though, democracy in ancient Athens grew out of conflicts within the nobility. Cleisthenes of Athens (*c.*570 BC–*c.*508 BC) was a scion of the Alcmaeonid family, prominent in politics since the 8th century BC. Cleisthenes (Figure 2) was named after his maternal grandfather Cleisthenes, Tyrant of Sicyon. Cleisthenes of Sicyon and Alcmaeon, who was the paternal grandfather of Cleisthenes of Athens, had been allies in a holy war to protect the Delphic Oracle. Victory was celebrated with the revival of the Pythian Games, at which Cleisthenes of Sicyon won the first chariot race in 582 BC. However, the

2. Cleisthenes of Sicyon at the Olympic Games.

Alcmaeonids had earlier been cursed on the advice of the Delphic Oracle and were twice exiled from Athens. Cleisthenes of Athens was able to return to Athens when he was about 45 and he was recorded as chief archon (magistrate) in 525–524 BC.

In 508 BC, there was conflict within the Athenian nobility about reforms that had been instituted by statesman and poet Solon (630–560 BC). Solon had replaced rule by the wealthy only with participation by farmers and smaller landowners. Cleisthenes gathered the support of the common people to institute further-reaching reforms by abolishing the principle of inherited privilege, which favored the conservative nobles. Instead, geographic localities became requirements for citizenship. Because more people could participate in political life, *isonomia*, equality of rights for all, was proclaimed. This change from family to locality as the basis of political representation earned Cleisthenes of Athens the enduring title of "founder of democracy"—in the West. However, the history of the origins of democracy reaches beyond the West.

The word *demokratia* (δημοκρατία), or rule by the *demos* or the people, first referred to the direct, participatory democracy of the city state of Athens, as instituted by Cleisthenes, and it later came to include the quasi-representative government of the Roman Republic. When democracy was successful in Greece and Rome, it was accompanied by political rhetoric that validated and glorified it, often as motivation for military action. The Greek people were proud of their *eleuthería* (ἐλευθερία) or freedom, and Romans had their *res publica*, or "people's thing." However, ancient democratic practices were not restricted to Athens and Rome but extended throughout Greece and other parts of the world. Still, despite the popularity of early democracy and its expanse, philosophers such as Plato, Aristotle, and Cicero were skeptical of rule by the people. Regardless, these critics also contributed to ideas about government and ethics that later became part of modern conceptions of democracy.

Democracy outside of Athens and Rome

Non-Eurocentric identifications of democracy in the ancient world have sometimes been part of political projects to claim democratic antecedents for places not previously considered democratic. Examples include democratic movements during the struggle for independence in India and more recent democratic movements in China. Resistance to Euro-centric views of the progress of Western civilization has also been part of multicultural efforts in the West, itself. For instance, Martin Bernal's 1991 *Black Athena: Afroasiatic Roots of Classical Civilization* attributed key cultural achievements of classical Greece to Egyptian influences in ways that supported African American and African diasporic reclamation of black history.

Historical research has identified democracy in Mesopotamia, including Assyria, Babylonia, Anatolia, Persia, and Sumeria (Anatolia is now Turkey and Persia is Iran; Assyria, Babylonia, and Sumeria are in Iraq). This form of governance consisted of deliberation in people's assemblies that influenced kings and sometimes had ultimate authority. Democratic influences from Phoenicia (now Lebanon and Syria) are believed to have inspired democratic innovations in parts of Greece, before Athenian democracy. All of the democratic structures in these areas probably spread through the mechanisms and requirements of trade, rather than explicit political ideology. Political structures in ancient Israel, northern India, and China also had democratic elements, as did the government of Sparta. These strains of democracy merit more detailed focus, to show that ancient democracy was not restricted to Athens and Rome.

The Amarna Letters, preserved on Egyptian clay tablets, recorded diplomatic reports of difficulties in dealing with Phoenician cities in the 1300s BC. Although, like Egypt, these cities were monarchies, they also had councils of elders and assemblies who sought to bypass their rulers and negotiate directly with the Egyptian pharaoh. These influential councils represented broader populations and persisted at least until the 10th century BC. The elders of Gebal/Byblos and other cities, such as Tyre, eventually became more powerful than the monarch. Carthage, originally a colony of Tyre, had a constitution requiring that the two suffetes, who were elected annually, govern on the advice of a council of elders. Carthage also had elections, town meetings, and trade guilds.

Greek historian Polybius (264–146 BC) suggested that Rome was able to conquer Carthage because Carthage's "measures were deliberated upon by the many." When Alexander the Great conquered Sidon, in 333 BC, the king surrendered because his citizens willed it; in Tyre, it was the people who refused entry to Alexander, and he vanquished the city. Phoenicians were influential when Homer produced the *Iliad* and probably during the Trojan War period in the 12th century BC. Homer referred to assemblies of elders, as well as kings. There is archaeological and textual evidence that before Athens became democratic, the city states of Chios, Erythrae, Chalcis, Naxos, Argos, Elis, Syracuse, and Acragas both traded with Phoenicians and had democratic practices themselves. Athens was surrounded by these other city states and interacted with them, so it is not a big leap to surmise that Athenian leaders were inspired by these nearby democratic practices.

Sparta was admired by Plato and Aristotle, among others, for its collective standards of self-discipline, military prowess, and egalitarianism in its elite classes, which included the education of women. Sparta's ruling and social system has been claimed throughout the centuries, by democrats, militarists, and in the 1930s, on account of its abolition of private property, by communists. Sparta had a mixed government that has confounded political theorists, but it is known that early on, about 750–600 BC, its constitution was democratic in specifying regular meetings for a popular assembly. At the same time, through reforms by Lycurgus (born *c*.800 BC), the power of Sparta's dual kingship was checked by popular election from within an expanding assembly to the *gerousia*, or council of elders. Over the following century, the assembly came to overrule the *gerousia* and appoint *ephors* who functioned first as judges over civil cases and then as executives within Sparta, who also conducted foreign relations. (Aristotle suggested that Sparta had been influenced by Carthage toward democracy, but Stephen Stockwell, co-editor of the 2011 *The Secret History of Democracy*, reasons that, more likely, Phoenicians influenced both Carthaginians and Spartans in this regard.)

There were also democratic assemblies outside of Greece and Phoenicia. Reports of democratic practices in both Israel and India were embedded in religious texts, which obscured their political content. The idea of a covenant between the people and God in ancient Israel, in addition to biblical reports of assemblies, looks like an early version of modern social contract theory, whereby the people have legitimate authority that precedes the authority of their rulers. (Modern social contract theory is the foundation of present constitutional democracies, as will be discussed in Chapter 4.) Contemporary Chinese scholars believe that in ancient China, during the Age of Confucius (c.1000–250 BC), the expression of moral expectations of bureaucratic officials was in itself democratic, even though these officials were selected based on merit.

There were democratic beliefs and practices during the Buddhist period in India (600 BC–AD 200). Government was dominated by a military caste from wealthy families, but castes were not rigidly demarcated then, and newly formed groups could demand political representation. The *Vishnu Purana* records that the Vajjian Confederacy in northern India was structured as a republic with representative government, during the 5th and 6th centuries BC. Nabhaga, the first king of Vaishali, the capital of the confederacy, was reported to have abdicated to further his people's interests and then said, "I am now a free tiller of the soil, king over my acre." (The archaeological ruins of Vaishali are now in Bihar State, India.)

Democracy in Athens and Rome

The city states of Athens and Rome are credited with the full-scale development of democracy. Democracy in Athens was direct or participatory, while democracy in Rome had the partially representative structure of a republic. Both Athenian and Roman democracy were dominated by elites and slavery was widely practiced. Indeed, the coexistence of democratic government and slavery persisted internationally until the mid-19th century. Ancient Greece and Rome had two of the five slave-dependent economies in recorded history (over 10 percent of national income dependent on slave labor)—the others were Brazil, the Caribbean, and the United States South. However, slavery is more persistent than large-scale economic dependence. Observers believe that there are 12–45 million slaves in the world today, more than ever existed. Many are women and children who are sexually exploited or kept in debts that are set up to be unpayable.

There is a consensus today that slavery is morally bad and modern states outlaw it. However, in ancient Greece and Rome, slavery was morally acceptable and legally administered. What conception of democracy could so easily coexist with slavery? It pertained to how the people participated in rule or government and restriction of membership in "the people" to male adult citizens who owned property or had served in the military. Foreigners, women, and manual workers, as well as slaves, were not members of "the people" and could not be citizens. Slaves were called *andrapoda* or "man-footed beasts" in Greek, from *tetrapoda* or four-footed beasts. In the *Code of Justinian*, compiled in the middle 6th century as a detailed overview of Roman law and its interpretations, Part V, "On Status" reads, "Now the main division of the law on persons is this, that all human beings are either free or slaves."

Slaves were generally contemned in the ancient world. About 800 years before the *Code of Justinian*, Aristotle defined slaves as suited for physical labor only, and incapable of the otherwise universal trait of reasoning. Nevertheless, in both Greece and Rome, slaves were soldiers, doctors, teachers, and artisans, as well as workers in agriculture and mining. The official derogatory descriptions of slaves may have provided a stereotype that justified continual enforcement and aimed to justify an institution that some implicitly believed required justification. Slave rebellion was a constant concern for the leadership classes of both Athens and Rome. In spring 72 BC, the escaped Thracian slave and gladiator Spartacus mustered a force of about 50,000 men. They won and lost battles with different parts of the Roman military, before their final defeat. To warn against future slave insurrections, the Romans crucified over 6,000 of Spartacus' forces, along the Appian Way. In both Athens and Rome, the fear and derogation of slaves was related to the jealous protection of social and political hierarchy.

The conception of democracy that is compatible with slavery is not our modern conception. In the ancient world, democracy was reserved for elites who were pushing up against more privileged elites who they thought were tyrants. Democracy as a system that includes the common people was looked down upon. Plato and Aristotle resolutely defended existing or remaining inequalities, particularly those based on virtuous character and intellectual merit, and including Greek nationality, good breeding, and male gender. In the *Republic*, Plato (*c.*428–348 BC) mocked the social equalities he associated with democracy. After pointing out that women would be equal to men in a democratic society, he went on:

> No one would believe how much freer the very beasts subject to men are in such a city than elsewhere. The dogs literally verify the adage and "like their mistresses become." And likewise the horses and asses are wont to hold on their way with the utmost freedom and dignity, bumping into everyone who meets them and who does not step aside. And so all things everywhere are just bursting with the spirit of liberty.

Aristotle (384–322 BC) was more subtle in his *Politics*, taking care to valorize changes in leadership positions among equal aristocratic rulers under aristocracy, or rule by an elite few, in a *polity*. At the same time, Aristotle presented universal direct democracy as the worst form of government: "Whereas oligarchy is characterised by birth, wealth, and education, the notes of democracy appear to be the opposite of these,—low birth, poverty, mean employment."

Both Plato and Aristotle were biased against democracy from their experience of the trial of Socrates. The death of Socrates, Plato's mentor, followed a jury verdict of 280–220 from 500 jurors who had been chosen by lot. Socrates had been tried for corrupting the youth of Athens by asking philosophical questions of experts which they could not answer, and he had a devoted following of aristocratic young men. After Socrates' death, Plato abandoned his political career in Athens. Aristotle studied in Plato's academy and then left for Macedonia to tutor Alexander the Great, who was then a boy of 13. When Aristotle returned to Athens, anti-Macedonian sentiment led to charges against him. Rather than stand trial, he fled, quipping that he "would not let the Athenians sin twice against philosophy."

Roman statesman Marcus Tullius Cicero (106–43 BC), like Aristotle and Plato, believed in a cyclical theory of government in which types of states degenerated into their opposites. He also took a dim view of direct participatory democracy, proclaiming in *De re publica* that "Democracy, while seemingly the most conducive to liberty, recognizes no distinctions between citizens and easily turns into mob-rule." Cicero concluded that democracy was the worst of the three simple types of government that included monarchy/tyranny, aristocracy/oligarchy, and democracy/ochlocracy.

We can make sense of this assessment of democracy by leading political theorists in the ancient world by remembering that their conception of what they called "democracy" was neither democratic rule among elites (which they did favor), nor representative government (not yet fully invented), but universal direct democracy. All who opposed democracy also strongly opposed tyranny and the institution of limited democracy among elites was consistent with that.

In the 6th and 7th centuries BC, the rulers of Athens were chief magistrates. Solon's reforms in 594 BC resulted in political participation in an *assembly* for free property owners, who became citizens. The *boule*, a council with 400 members, 100 from each of four tribes, functioned as the government. Peisistratus overthrew this government, replacing it with a brutal tyranny. But the democratic government was reinstated and that was when Cleisthenes was charged with designing reforms (in 508–507 BC). He instituted a massive reorganization into 139 demes, each with 150–250 members. Ten new tribes replaced the previous four and all male citizens over 18 were registered and obligated to participate in the government; each tribe could select 50 by lot, as members of a Council of 500 that administered the city.

Athens retained this assembly form of government, but the power of leading aristocratic families was weakened. The change did not occur as a matter of democratic principle, but because, as someone known as "The Old Oligarch" put it, helmsmen, boatswains, junior officers, and shipwrights were needed for the navy in ongoing conflicts with Persia. The great orator-statesman Pericles (495–429 BC) expanded democracy during the Peloponnesian War (that some said he incited). Defeat by Sparta in the Peloponnesian War, in 404 BC, brought the rule of the "Thirty Tyrants" for a year. Athenian democracy faltered further following defeats from Philip II of Macedon in 338 BC, and eventually Athens was subsumed under the Roman Republic.

The Roman Republic came into existence after overthrow of the Etruscan monarchy in 509 BC. It was termed a *rēspūblica*, a "thing" that belonged to the Roman people. In reality it was *Senatus Populusque Romanus*, SPQR, The Senate and the People of Rome. The Roman people were citizens by birth, naturalization, or manumission from slavery. Compared to Athens, where only native-born residents could be citizens, citizenship was greatly expanded. Assemblies met in the Forum and participation was therefore not possible for those outside of the city—the election of representatives had not been invented—although the assemblies were supposed to collectively represent all citizens. There were four assemblies or councils, made up of local groups from ancient tribes, military units, the common people, and an assembly that all citizens could attend. However, these assemblies were not as powerful as the Senate, which was composed of members of aristocratic families. The assemblies elected the chief administrative officers, two consuls, who concurrently served for one year and could not serve the following year. This political structure sustained much internal dispute and intrigue over power. Soon after Julius Caesar was assassinated in 44 BC, Rome became an empire, with a succession of emperors.

The government structures of both Athens and Rome, as well as earlier forms of democratic rule, originated and changed, as the result of both internal competition and external pressures. Although the democratic idea of a division of power within government was not explicitly formulated in the ancient world, it already existed in the divided structures that developed to share power, such as Phoenician elders and kings, the Athenian boule and assembly, or the Roman configuration of assemblies, senate, and consuls. Thus, conceptions of democracy in the ancient world included government with divided powers that could act as a check on absolute rule concentrated in the authority of one or a very few. But government could be democratic only within itself, without extending democratic participation to the majority of residents, that is, to society.

Democratic innovations from ancient critics

Despite their opposition to universal direct participatory democracy, Plato, Aristotle, and Cicero provided theories of government and human nature that were important contributions to democratic political theory in later times. Plato and Aristotle between them invented ethics as standards and practices of right and wrong that were independent of religion and custom, and Cicero introduced political principles that would be reiterated and put into practice in modernity.

Socrates was Plato's inspirational teacher and the main character in many of his dialogues. In the dialogue *Euthyphro*, Socrates is on the way to his own trial. He encounters Euthyphro, a priest who is prosecuting his own father for murder. Euthyphro is confident that his action is supported by religion, but Socrates confounds him with the following (rephrased) dilemma: Is a morally good action good because the gods love it, or do they love it because it is already good? The first reason is arbitrary, because the gods disagreed in ancient times, and today there are different religions. The second reason implies that there is a standard apart from what the gods or God love(s) and we can have direct access to that standard, without gods, God, or religion. As set up, this dilemma separates morality from religion and it has implications for any political system presented as morally good or right. It grounds both the modern idea of separation of church and state, and with that, a government that is religiously neutral or completely secular.

In *The Republic*, Plato advocated rule by the best in society, who had both wisdom and experience, and were dedicated to taking care of those over whom they ruled. He argued for a specialized political class of rulers, analogous to doctors or sea captains. Plato's idea of rulers' expertise and knowledge endures today in ideas that government officials should make decisions based on evidence and science. His idea of care of those governed persists in democratic ideals of dedicated public service. Both expert rule and public service suggest the need for a class of political professionals, which is different from rule by anyone in society or rule by those with only wealth and leisure.

Aristotle asserts in *The Politics* that man is a political animal, "by nature." Man is normally political, because the normal man is within the state that is itself a creation of nature. Anyone without a state is either bad or above humanity. In his *Nicomachean Ethics*, Aristotle explains the virtues or traits of character that

29

enable the well-born to live happy lives. Virtues are neither determined by nature nor precluded by nature. Aristotle's account of virtues, which includes courage and temperance, with an emphasis on generosity and magnanimity, describes the virtues of privileged aristocrats—women, children, and slaves, those in great misery, or who are ugly or poor, cannot be virtuous. However, contra Aristotle, the practice of acquiring virtues of character is, in principle, inclusive, because reason makes it possible to be virtuous, and reason is universal according to what is now known about human nature, aptitude, and capability.

One acquires a virtue by first knowing what it is and practicing it in real life occasions that one recognizes as calling for that virtue. The development of a virtue requires practical judgment and use of the practical syllogism that ends in the relevant action. This process is cumulative. For example, one is courageous if one resolves to be courageous, and for that reason decides upon and performs courageous acts. Over time one's courageous acts come from a disposition to perform them, because one has performed them in the past. Aristotle's psychological technology is an important contribution to democratic equality because all rational humans can apply it to what they accept or create as virtues.

Civic participation is a virtue according to Aristotle, so that ethics loops back into politics. Aristotle was also aware of the importance of liberty (*eleutheria*), so that "a man should live as he likes" (unless he is a slave). He associated this kind of liberty with democracy's "claim of men to be ruled by none, if possible." But Aristotle also specified that if impossible, the alternative is to rule and be ruled in turns, which he associated with aristocracy as a form of government. To live as one likes and be ruled in turns is now associated with democracy. The freedom and civic participation that Aristotle reserved for aristocrats among themselves has been extended to broader populations in contemporary conceptions of democracy.

Cicero is famous for expressing cosmopolitan views about the unity of humankind. At the beginning of *On Obligations/De Officiis*, he wrote: "Nature...joins individuals together, enabling them by the power of reason to share a common language and life." He relied on an idea of higher law to uphold the value of "human fellowship," although he acknowledged that besides the level "shared by the human race without limit," there are closer ties based on race, nation, language, residence, friendship, and family. Cicero generally described the state as a gathering of people who agree to laws in the expectation of benefits—an idea that pre-dated later social contract theory (see Chapter 4). In *De Legibus*, he asserted that government was based on the authority of the people, so that it had a duty to fulfil individual strivings for excellence. Cicero also posited the independence of ethics and law, because each was derived separately from natural or higher law. This meant that, unlike Plato and Aristotle, Cicero clearly distinguished between society and government, with ethics belonging to society and law to government. (This distinction is important for considering modern progressive programs to democratize society, under democratic government (see Chapter 6).) He also stressed the obligation of government to protect private property (*On Obligations*, 6 (book I, 11)). Despite these proto-democratic notes, like Aristotle, Cicero was talking to aristocrats about how they should govern and be governed.

These ideas from the political theories of Plato, Aristotle, and Cicero were more general than their derogatory assessments of universal participatory democracy, which arose from their privileged perspectives in concrete political and social circumstances. The ideas of informed and dedicated secular government officials, the universal rational ability for citizens to participate in government as the result of their character, a perspective of human unity, and the concept of government as obligated to benefit those governed, were all visionary and aspirational in ways that would inform conceptions of democracy in future history. Some of the subsequent thought was directly influenced by classical sources, but as theorists and activists formed new conceptions of democracy, even though their ideas resembled these ideas from the ancient world, they could be presented and received as original in their own times.

Chapter 3
Democracy in the medieval and Renaissance world

Neither feminism nor democracy as we now know them flourished during the Middle Ages. But on a feminist note, history and cinema still celebrate Joan of Arc (1412–31) and Queen Elizabeth I (1533–1603). Joan of Arc (Figure 3), who led French forces against the English during the Hundred Years War, was executed mainly for the heresy of dressing like a man; Queen Elizabeth, who successfully toyed with suitors for political ends, presided over England's ascension in trade, military might, and literature. Contemporary feminist scholars have revisited the careers of both.

Medieval Europe lacked national democratic government structures and ideals. Monarchs ruled by divine right and although slavery was largely replaced with serfdom, it was still not against the law and was widely practiced. (Even the Catholic Church owned slaves.) However, there were democratic assemblies throughout regions that would become parts of more modern nations and the Magna Carta was instituted in 1215. Both Catholic dominance and the Protestant Reformation produced theology and doctrine that affirmed individual rights, which came to be elements of modern conceptions of democracy. Also, democratic ideas that began in theological contexts were expressed in secular form during the Renaissance period. The revival of classical learning would not have been possible without freedoms associated with democratic society, although they were, of course,

Joan at the walls of Paris

3. "Joan at the walls of Paris", *c.*1860. Joan of Arc (*c.*1412–31), also known as The Maid of Orléans, took part in the siege of Paris in 1429. From *The Comic History of England*, Volume I, by Gilbert A. A'Beckett (London: Bradbury, Agnew, and Co.).

checked by the Inquisition—we need think only of Galileo's house arrest for asserting that the Earth revolves around the Sun, and not vice versa.

Democratic practices during medieval and Renaissance times

Democratic practices during the medieval and Renaissance period were not generally based on abstract principles. Rather, they were the results of concrete negotiations to resolve conflicting interests. For instance, without fully developed contract law, there were contractual agreements during feudalism, so that tenants were subject to forfeiture for not fulfilling their parts of bargains with lords and they could withdraw allegiance (at least in principle) if the lord defaulted.

The English Magna Carta of June 15, 1215 was originally signed by King John to address decades-long grievances from a group of barons. At issue were royal decrees of taxation and military service for the Third Crusade and French wars. This first Magna Carta was soon repudiated by John, but it was continually reissued and reaffirmed, until parliament was firmly established as a legislative branch of government in the late 17th century. During that process, the Magna Carta came to be interpreted as a set of principles that applied not only to the original barons, but to all citizens. Individual freedom and trial by jury, as well as the idea of a "community of the realm" that is represented by republican government, were vouchsafed in articles 39 and 61 of the Magna Carta. In principle, the Magna Carta brought the monarchy under the rule of law and upheld the legal rights of citizens.

The Magna Carta itself was pre-dated by earlier checks on the powers of rulers in England and Europe. Historians point to democratic antecedents in the institution of advisers to 6th- and 7th-century Anglo-Saxon kings. And, by the 9th and 10th centuries, assemblies had developed that included landowners and clergy. After the Norman Conquest of 1066, both the nobility and clergy upheld the laws of the kings, throughout England. Kings called Great Councils of the archbishops, bishops, abbots, barons, and earls who locally upheld the feudal system. This representative arrangement did not always function harmoniously. Disagreements between the crown and clergy could bring the government to a halt and internal opposition could be brutally crushed. In 1170, Thomas Becket, Archbishop of Canterbury, was assassinated after his long dispute with Henry II over church jurisdiction.

Democratic institutions persisted or developed during the medieval and Renaissance period throughout Europe, in

Scandinavia, France, Germany, and Italy, as well as England. Scandinavian assemblies of residents were often called words translated as "things" in English, reminiscent of the Roman *res publica* meaning "people's thing." The organization of the Icelandic "Althing" was structured with law-making and juridical powers. It met yearly and contained 48 voting members of the Law Council that had legislative powers. New laws were made, fines and punishments set, and banishments reviewed. The four quarters of Iceland also held local assemblies and had courts that met at the Althing that also appointed judges from among local farmers.

In Denmark, Norway, and Sweden, during the Viking Age (783–1066), "things" were assemblies of concerned clan members who met to resolve disputes, assert their interests through "lawspeakers," and solemnize important events and agreements. While deliberations within these "things" had scant influence or effect beyond their participants, they were practices of shared power based on local discussion. Where there were "things," the governance of a community was not a simple matter of one person asserting their wishes over everyone else. Still, these "things" were likely to have been dominated by those individuals and families who were already influential and wealthy.

In early 14th-century France, the Parlement of Paris developed from the King's Council that had jurisdiction over the whole country. Parliaments in distinct regions with historical independence from the monarchy were recognized on a national level by the 15th century. For instance, in 1443, the region of Languedoc-Roussillon in southern France became ruled by the Parlement of Toulouse. After the Hundred Years War (1337–1453), Grenoble, Bordeaux, Dijon, and Rouen also established *parlements* that were made part of France by 1500. Still, the emergence of these *parlements* was less a sharing of national power and reflected more the failure of the French government to centralize. The regional *parlements* were called in by the monarchy to serve its interests, rather than assert their own.

The growth of French royal power had by 1300 resulted in a general assembly made up of church officials and secular lords and representatives from some towns, but its main purpose was to provide funds for the crown. After his dispute with Pope Boniface VIII, in 1302, Philip IV (Philip the Fair) summoned the assembly of the Estates-General of clergy, nobility, and commoners, but only the representatives of the Third Estate of commoners were elected in the towns they represented, while country districts had no representation. Unlike the Scandinavian "things," France's medieval form of assembly and representation did extend beyond the membership of assemblies, although it was not based on what would later be called democratic principles of federal or republican government. The contrast is whether assemblies were voluntary associations for the benefit of those assembled, as they were in Scandinavia, or, as in France, obligatory representation before a greater power, to serve that power.

Medieval democratic structures in Switzerland and Italy were independent, before their nation states were formed. Beginning in the 8th century, democracy in Switzerland developed steadily from a public voting system caried by the majority. This *Landsgemeinde*, or canton assembly, was especially prevalent in rural cantons. By the 13th century, the older "blood court" community decisions on punishment for crimes were replaced with more formal structures. When Switzerland became a federal state in 1848, central government replaced the authority of the *Landsgemeinde*. The 19th-century unification of Italy was similarly based on older structures of self-rule in city states. However, during the late medieval period, many of the Italian city states were republics unto themselves. Their populations were highly literate and numerate, with expertise in trade, crafts, and arts. Competition and warfare among them precluded Italian centralization until 1860.

In 962, Otto I, King of Germany, was crowned Holy Roman Emperor. By the 13th century, Germany was the largest part of the Holy Roman Empire. Until the 16th century, the emperor was elected by the highest-ranking nobles, although the empire itself never became a centralized federal system. The hundreds of kingdoms, principalities, duchies, counties, prince-bishoprics, and "free imperial cities" practiced only nominal allegiance as vassals to the emperor and generally functioned as independent sovereignties. In 1806, the Holy Roman Empire was officially dissolved. Nevertheless, its historical stages were forms of proto-federalism, toward modern federalism with central governments that have delineated powers according to constitutional law. The Holy Roman Empire, encompassing Germany, Austria, France, Italy, Belgium, Luxembourg, Switzerland, and Poland, has been considered an antecedent to the 20th-century European Union.

There were also medieval democratic institutions for governance outside of Europe, in Africa, Mexico, and the Middle East. Some of this history has been compiled only recently, due to a lack of written records. For instance, the Intangible Cultural Project of the United Nations Educational, Scientific, and Cultural Organization has curated the Kurukan Fuga charter of 1236, known as the Manden Charter. This was the constitution of the Mali Empire in west Africa and its goal was to regulate relations between different social groups toward stability and peace. Women and slaves were included as citizens and all citizens had equal rights.

According to a contemporaneous account, in Tlaxcallan, Mexico, mid-13th-century candidates for the senate, who were already proven warriors, were subjected to attacks by a crowd before entering a temple where priests would teach them the legal and moral code. This two-year course of study, under the power of the people, included starvation, whippings, and self-administered bloodletting. Recent archaeological evidence suggests a collective society without a powerful leader in Tlaxcallan. One hundred senators made ultimate political and military decisions, but the common people influenced the government that had withstood attacks from autocratic Tenochtitlan, the capital of the Mexica Empire.

Contemporary Islamic scholars have claimed that after the death of Muhammad, a new order of society and government developed under the Umayyad dynasty, during the Rashidun Caliphate in the 7th century. Earlier tribalism had democratic practices, but now, government was based on principles of consultation, consensus, elections, and independent reasoning. All humans were to have rights and protections, fair treatment in the courts, and equal opportunity, as well as property rights. In accord with the Quran, there was to be no hierarchy within the clergy and religious freedom was espoused. While these political principles were accompanied by religious obligations to pray and fast, in practical social terms, they were also inclusive. The same freedoms were extended to the poor, slaves, and members of non-Muslim minority communities. Rulers were elected collectively, and women voted.

Democratic thought during the medieval and Renaissance periods

From its beginning, Christianity promised equality, but this was either equality in spirit or equality in the afterlife. Actual physical life in the here and now was left out. Church Father St Augustine (354–430) tried to reconcile real inequalities by positing equality under God as a religious principle and Heaven as a real place (albeit after death). In his *Confessions* (*c*.400) Augustine followed St Paul in separating the Christian mind-soul from the physical body, reserving morality and unity with God for the former, only. In *City of God* (*c*.413–26), Augustine claimed that God did not condone either human slavery or autocratic rule, but he did not mention great inequalities in wealth. (St Ambrose (340–97), also a church Father, had advocated limits on private property so that some things would be "common.") Augustine also said that slavery was just punishment for sinners, or as a just alternative to being killed by victors in a war. (This just-war argument was to be philosopher John Locke's main justification for slavery in the 17th century—see Chapter 4.)

By the 13th century, the esteemed theologian and scholar St Thomas Aquinas (1225–74) adroitly reasoned that slaves were already free in having autonomy over their private lives, including diet and marriage (*Summa Theologica*, II-IIQ104, 1265–74). It is not evident what form of slavery Aquinas had in mind, because slave owners have typically controlled what slaves eat and with whom they procreate. However, Christian attempts to reconcile equal freedom and slavery implied assumptions that there was, or ought to be, universal human equality, or at least that slavery was wrong. The idea of universal human equality was only first explicitly promulgated in the 1948 United Nations Universal Declaration of Human Rights, and that was a secular formulation (see Appendix).

Democratic medieval political thought was bound up with religion. During the Carolingian Renaissance of the Court of Charlemagne in the late 8th and early 9th centuries, Rabanus Maurus (780–856), Jonas of Orléans (780–842), and Hincmar of Reims (806–82) wrote about the difference between just kingship and unjust tyranny. They held that as a religious official, the king should be instructed by the clergy. The king was obligated to be just, in accordance with law that was made up of tradition, the king's decrees, and popular consent. Kings who acted unlawfully, without popular consent, could be deposed.

Both Catholic doctrine and the new ideas of the Protestant Reformation contributed to what would later be abstract theories of democratic national government. In the 13th century, St Thomas Aquinas wrote that rulers ought to be elected and that they could be removed if unjust, thereby implying both the ultimate political power of the people and a contract between rulers and ruled. The church held its power to be superior to the power of secular government. Within the church, the feudal aristocracy carried out church policies, and there was also local representation. Some theologians argued for democracy within the church. Marsilius of Padua claimed that all monarchs, including the pope, represented the people as sovereign. Marsilius claimed in *Defensor Pacis* that the people had a right to vote for members of representative councils. Nicholas of Cusa, who was appointed Vicar General of the Papal States, proposed a democratic method for electing the pope. Nicholas's plan was not accepted by the church, but it later came to be used in institutions as the "Borda Count" that allows voters to rank leaders or preferences, resulting in a single winner.

Several Catholic medieval scholars contested the doctrine of church theologians. William of Ockham objected to Aquinas' reliance on natural law, because it conflicted with biblical ideas of God's freedom and omnipotence. (That is, if God were perfectly free, he could not also be subject to natural law.) In his *Work of Ninety Days*, published in about 1333, he supported private property by arguing that although common ownership or use was justified before the Fall, after the Fall there had been private property agreements that it was morally right to honor. (The subject of private property was to play a major role in 17th- and 18th-century social contract theory, as well as the founding of the United States constitution (as will be discussed in Chapters 4 and 5).) Ockham also objected to unrestricted papal power, in favor of the freedom of citizens.

Protestantism directly challenged papal power. Martin Luther (1483–1546) emphasized the importance of secular political power. Calvinist ministers were themselves elected. In *Franco Gallia* (1573), French Protestant lawyer François Hotman (1524–90) argued historically, with reference to the French

Assembly of Estates, for representative government and elected monarchy. Protestantism generally emphasized the importance of the individual's direct relationship to God, without the intermediary of priests or ministers, perhaps pre-dating the modern political emphasis on individual rights. Differences in religious belief between monarchs and subjects led Catholics to limit their obedience to Protestant monarchs and Protestants to emphasize popular sovereignty against Catholic monarchs.

Finally, Niccolò di Bernardo dei Machiavelli (1469–1527), while notorious for prescribing manipulative statecraft in *The Prince* (1513), was a staunch defender of republicanism in *The Discourses on Livy* (published posthumously in 1531), and he was generally critical of Christianity. Referring to the Roman Republic, he argued that the greatness of a state depended on the *virtù* of its citizens, consisting of their strength, ability, and civic virtue. Machiavelli insisted that citizen participation in a government was necessary for its stability, although he cautioned that emergencies might require autocracy.

The importance of these democratic precursors

The medieval and Renaissance period had enough democratic practices and thought to keep the tradition alive and advance it. For example, the idea of a contract or compact between citizens and government, traceable from Cicero through the Renaissance, provides for government accountability. Effective demands that the government answer to those governed became very important in historical events and conceptions of democracy in the early modern and modern periods. This accountability of government officials was not perfected until there were national constitutions setting out rules for what officials could and could not do. But those democratic national structures relied on democratic traditions from the medieval and Renaissance world.

The relation of democratic institutions on local levels to the emergence of national democracies can be studied through specific histories. More abstractly, democracy theorists have recently engaged in a "sequencing debate" that has special implications for emerging nations, as well as historical understanding. One side insists that nation states must exist before they can function as democracies. The other side makes a case that democratic institutions have preceded and facilitated national democracies. For instance, Danish political scientist Jørge Møller argues that the contrast in modern democratic structures between Russia and other European countries is related to the presence or absence of strong local democratic institutions, such as parliaments and assemblies. Møller draws on Max Weber's contrast between impersonal bureaucratic government and patrimonial government based on personal patronage and affiliation. When England, France, Spain, and other European nations became democratic, the process was enabled by traditions of parliaments and assemblies holding rulers accountable, impersonally, through laws. In Russia, however, despite top-down tsarist efforts to set up local organizations, there was no earlier tradition of actual accountability to parliament or local assemblies. In the absence of such prior institutional accountability, later accountability did not emerge, and neither did democracy.

The widespread medieval pattern of democratic institutions on local levels did not add up to national democracies, except perhaps in Switzerland. Histories or traditions of democratic institutions might be necessary for the formation of democratic national governments, but they are not sufficient, because even democracies themselves fail and not all regions with democratic institutions become democratic states, or parts of them. Also, it would be onerous to conclude that centuries of prior local practice are required before new democratic states can emerge, or existing states can become democratic. It might be tempting to describe such democratic history as "culture" and conclude that some cultures are more fertile for growing democracy than others. However, cultures, as well as governments, can change and become more democratic, or less so.

The difference between an obligatory assembly whose members are summoned in service to a higher power and a voluntary assembly in service to its members is important for assessing how "democratic" any particular democratic institution has been or is. Representation alone has not always been accompanied by political power. This was evident in medieval France and may continue in contemporary politics, anywhere. Also, local self-enclosed or isolated self-rule, while allowing for autonomy within a particular unit, does not provide democratic influence within larger political units that affect the autonomous units. A political unit, like a person, can be autonomous internally or autonomous in dealings with an external unit. The democratic principle of consent to government by those governed was evident even under feudalism, but the idea of real checks on national governing power awaited the 17th century and the reality of it, the 18th century. It is also important to distinguish between democratic antecedents after the fact and deliberately intended democracy, based on ideals and principles of governance. Democratic antecedents, like all tradition, may move forward because people are attached to what is familiar and adverse to change, whereas deliberate intentions are autonomous. A democratic spirit requires commitment or reaffirmation.

In the 20th and 21st centuries, African American scholars, activists in Latin America, contemporary political observers, and cultural anthropologists have stressed the importance of education for citizens in democracies. They follow in a tradition of advocacy for informed citizenry that began in the ancient world and was emphasized in the 18th and 19th centuries. But there is a difference between just limiting political participation to those who are already literate and expanding literacy. Literacy throughout Europe expanded along with the success of

Protestantism during the medieval period. The invention of the printing press by Johannes Gutenberg in the late 1430s supported the spread of literacy in Germany and with that, Protestantism, civic participation, and the education of women. Moreover, evidence of democratic institutions outside of Europe during the medieval period, as well as in the ancient world, suggests that such institutions could be universal in the future.

Chapter 4
The social contract: consent of those governed

Thomas Hobbes's *Leviathan* supported absolute monarchy. He was also widely known for believing that everything could be explained by "matter in motion," a materialist view that struck many as atheistic, because God and souls were nonmaterial. Members of the British parliament were so incensed by Hobbes's ideas that when he fled abroad, they burned him in effigy. Hobbes knew all of the major intellectuals in England and Europe and was well regarded by them. But after he taught himself mathematics, he was mocked when he thought he could square the circle. Hobbes was thus controversial, as both a philosopher and a man. Locke's reputation was more staid by comparison, although Rousseau also drew extreme reactions. All three found it wise to go abroad when their ideas showed a potential to put them in danger.

By the beginning of the 18th century, the idea of the *social contract* was accepted as a core of modern conceptions of democratic national government. Thomas Hobbes, John Locke, and Jean-Jacques Rousseau created the modern theory of the social contract, although they did not call their political philosophy "democratic." Unlike ancient and medieval political theorists, who analyzed existing forms of government, all three posited and justified forms of government that did not yet exist, in ways that were directly relevant to their own historical circumstances. That is striking for its note of activism submerged in political theory. The social contract was first envisioned as an agreement among a people to set up their government, but over time it came to refer to an agreement between people and their government.

The driving insight of the social contract was that legitimate government required the consent of those governed. This meant that the people, being rational about their self-interest, believed they were better off with government than without it. Thus, underlying the social contract was an idea of individual freedom and worth—without government, the people were free to grant or withhold consent to government and they had a right to improve their lives, which government would help them do. This idea of original freedom was derived from *natural law*, God's laws to mankind. God ordered the universe and determined the nature of everything in it, including man. Hobbes emphasized the freedom of humans to harm one another. Rousseau proclaimed, "Man is born free" in the first sentence of his 1762 *The Social Contract*. Locke followed Christian theologians in viewing man as created by God, in His image. (Scripture provided explicit support: "We are all equally made in God's image" (Genesis 1:26–8).) By the 18th century, individual worth could be asserted in secular terms. Philosopher Immanuel Kant held that humans had intrinsic worth, because their subjective consciousness made their lives valuable to them—although he was also a Christian.

Historical context

Central democratic governments are parts of nations. (Logically, democratic national government presupposes the existence of nations.) The social contract theorists wrote on the crest of turbulent political life in their times and they had national government in mind. Social contract theory offered both a new idea about the best form of government and narratives about how government came about in the first place.

The Peace of Westphalia followed periods of anarchic religious warfare, particularly the Thirty Years War (1618–48) that resulted in 4.5 to 8 million deaths over Central Europe, although most from disease and starvation. The 1648 Treaty of Westphalia sought to preserve the peace through an agreed-upon doctrine about nations: individual nation states were sovereign, nation states would respect each other's borders, and nation states could autonomously regulate themselves within their own borders. There was no plenary session for national delegations who subscribed to the Treaty of Westphalia. Signing on in stages, the treaty's signatories were France, Sweden, the Imperial Delegation (Germany), Spain, the Papal Nuncio, the Dutch Republic, and the Swiss Confederacy. England, Poland, Russia, and the Ottoman Empire were not signatories, but the Treaty of Westphalia settled the very idea of European nations.

It is not surprising that England was not a signatory to the Treaty of Westphalia, because the English Civil War that began in 1642 saw the execution of King Charles I, Oliver Cromwell's Protectorate, and the exile of King James II. Decades of unrest were punctuated by bubonic plague in 1665 and the Great Fire of London a year later. International rivalry and warfare between Protestant and Catholic countries fueled internal dispute. England had been officially Protestant since Henry VIII made himself Supreme Head of the Church of England in 1534. But there was intense religious strife within England, motivated by extreme Protestant suspicion of Catholic leanings by Charles I, who had sought to impose his Bible on Scotland. The monarchy required funding to put down rebellions in Ireland and Scotland, but it could only be provided by parliament, which was increasingly independent, and armed.

Cromwell rose to power as a general in parliament's army. But Protestants also had internal divisions. For instance, Levellers gained voice in seeking to expand suffrage for male property owners during the 1640s, although Cromwell had at least three of their leaders executed. The political movement of the Levellers advocated religious tolerance, but unlike the Diggers (who claimed to be the True Levellers), they were not in favor of involuntary communal ownership of property. This period of the English Civil War resolved into a limited and Protestant monarchy with strong parliament, when William and Mary were proclaimed king and queen in 1689. Religious rivalry no longer motivated political violence, although religious tolerance did not extend to Catholics.

Social contract theories

Thomas Hobbes (1588–1679) and John Locke (1632–1704), the two leading 17th-century English social contract theorists, were directly involved in the politics of their time. Hobbes was a royalist in accord with the views of his lifelong patrons, the Cavendish family. Locke was an advocate for representative government for the rising non-noble aristocracy and he was directly involved in justifying the Glorious Revolution of 1688 that restored Protestant rule to the British throne. Jean-Jacques Rousseau (1712–78) was not directly involved in politics. His approach to political philosophy was less about government structure and rights under government and more about the use of government to correct how society had corrupted human nature. He was also a novelist and he studied human psychology.

In his 1672 autobiography, Hobbes related how his birth in 1588 coincided with the approach of the Spanish Armada to the coast of England. He wrote, "Mother dear did bring forth twins at once, both me and fear." Hobbes was educated at Oxford and soon after became a tutor and later a secretary to the Cavendish family. When Charles II was in exile in Paris, Hobbes occasionally tutored him in mathematics. However, Hobbes was not a consistent royalist and, at different times, he managed to incur the wrath of both Tories and Whigs. His metaphysical materialism that reduced everything that existed, including the Christian soul, to matter in motion, fueled his reputation as an atheist, even though he consistently referred to God throughout his writings. Enemies in the Catholic Church and Oxford wanted to ban and burn his books and he himself burned his papers in reaction to a bill to suppress atheism. Despite parliament burning him in effigy, Hobbes lived to play tennis and write love poems in old age and he published his Latin verse autobiography at age 84.

In *Leviathan* (1651), Hobbes presented his idea of a sovereign as an overriding, ultimate force. But he broke with the royalist idea of rule by divine right and instead insisted that sovereignty was made legitimate by consent of those ruled. The chief obligation of the sovereign was to protect subjects and Hobbes asserted their right to reject a sovereign who failed to do this: "A subject has no obligation to obey a sovereign if he judges that the sovereign is not providing for his security." Hobbes based this need for protection by powerful government on his description of "the state of nature," the human condition without or before government.

Along with other social contract theorists, Hobbes posited the "state of nature" as variably a literal time in early human history or a thought experiment used to justify a certain kind of government. To describe conditions of life in the state of nature, it was necessary to put forth a theory of human nature. Hobbes did not believe that human beings were naturally sociable, and he thought that the variety of their wants precluded a common good. Humans sought one another out only for glory, competition, or to band together out of fear. Hobbes described the state of nature as a condition of war, like fear itself, in which each was against all, as a whole and one by one. The weakest could kill the strongest and no one was safe. Violent death was universally feared and preemptive action was always possible.

The first Right of Nature was self-preservation, based on universal reason. The primary rational arrangement in human interactions and transactions was the contract or compact. But if one party performed their part of a contract, in the state of nature, there was no way to guarantee that the other side would keep their part of the bargain. To remedy this general natural situation in which life was "nasty, poor, brutish, and short," Hobbes speculated that "men," or the people, agreed among themselves to give up their power to harm one another and place all destructive force in the hands of the sovereign. Hobbes's social contract was an agreement among the people to make an irrevocable gift of their natural right to use force for self-preservation, to the Leviathan. Thus, the social contract was:

> [A] covenant of every man with everyman, as though every man should say to every man, *I authorize and give up my right of governing myself to this man, or to this assembly of men, on this condition, that thou give up thy right to him, and authorize all his actions in like manner.*

It is important to recognize that this was not a contract between the people and the government. Rather, it was an irrevocable gift of everyone's individual power to a sovereign who would then have the power to enforce all contracts and keep the peace.

Hobbes went on to describe such legitimate government as controlling everything, including the press, religion, and all of the institutional agreements necessary for civilized society in which business could be conducted and culture develop. There could be no justice without the laws that issued from the sovereign and no other way to obey the First Law of Nature, which was, Seek peace. Hobbes had laid the groundwork for *Leviathan* in his first and second editions of *De Cive* (*On the Citizen*) (1642/7), where he claimed that reason provides a maxim "to fly a contra-natural dissolution, as the greatest mischief that can arrive to nature." He further claimed that great societies did not originate "in the mutual good will men had towards each other, but in the mutual fear that they had of each other." And furthermore, this fear is not momentary fright, but "a certain foresight of future evil."

This foresight that would motivate preemptive violence was quelled when all force was mutually relinquished to the sovereign. That is, the peace provided by Hobbes's strong government included the peace of mind from a feeling of safety.

However, there were limits to the powerful rights of the Leviathan and natural rights prevailed, even under strong government. Thus, Hobbes insisted that certain rights, such as self-defense and rights to liberty in movement and life functions, could not be taken away from individuals. It may seem contradictory to posit an all-powerful—what we would call "totalitarian"—sovereign and also insist on individual rights. But Hobbes's motive for the all-powerful sovereign can be understood as desire for protection of individual life and liberty (Figure 4). And although he was not

4. *Leviathan* of Hobbes after stamp from the 17th century. Drawing by Abraham Bosse. *Leviathan or The Matter, Forme and Power of a Common-Wealth Ecclesiasticall and Civil*—commonly referred to as *Leviathan*—is a book written by Thomas Hobbes (1588–1679) and published in 1651 (revised Latin edition 1668).

overly concerned with exactly how much liberty needed to be exchanged for safety, he did not go so far as to say, as Rousseau would, that one should not resist a death sentence.

Locke was at the prestigious Westminster School when Charles I was executed in 1649. He may have had royalist sympathies in his youth, but his father fought in Cromwell's cavalry. After leaving Oxford University, he became involved in the pro-parliament political activities of Lord Anthony Ashley-Cooper, later Earl of Shaftesbury. Their relationship was cemented early on when Locke, who had a medical degree, oversaw a complex, dangerous, and ultimately successful operation of inserting a silver pipette into an abscess on Ashley-Cooper's liver. Locke served as Ashley-Cooper's physician, secretary, and political representative, from 1668 until Shaftesbury's death in 1683. During that time Ashley-Cooper was made Secretary of the Board of Trade and Plantations and Secretary to the Lords Proprietors of the Carolinas. Locke is believed to have co-written, with Ashley-Cooper, the constitution for that colony, which approved slavery.

Locke's *Second Treatise of Government* was widely received as a foundational social contract text for modern democratic government. Although Locke used neither the word "contract" nor "democracy" in his political writing, his religious and moral justification of property rights and insistence on a representative legislature galvanized democratic planners in the American and French Revolutions, as well as England's Glorious Revolution in his own time. Indeed, Locke accompanied Mary when she sailed from Holland to become queen, in 1689. Mary II was the daughter of James II, who had been deposed for his conflicts with parliament and for accepting Catholicism in England, as well as France. The new king and queen ruled jointly. As a staunch Protestant, William of Orange had been invited by prominent Protestants to invade England in 1688, but he did not want to assume the throne as a conqueror and insisted that Mary share it with him.

Locke's *Second Treatise* was first published in 1689, but it is believed to have been written and parts of it circulated within Shaftesbury's circle, during the preceding 20 years. In contrast to Hobbes, Locke had a benign theory of human nature in the state of nature and the main purpose of government was not protection from "contra-natural dissolution," but the protection of private property. Still, like Hobbes, Locke reserved the right of the people to rebel if their government failed to protect them. Locke's state of nature, without real political power or government, was a condition of life in which men, created by God, obeyed the Law of Nature. This was a rational principle that "teaches all mankind who will but consult it, that being all equal and independent, no one ought to harm another in his life, health, liberty or possessions." Still, liberty was not license, because no one, as God's creature, was free to destroy himself.

Considerable cooperation and even commerce were possible in the state of nature according to Locke. But there were the inconveniences of a lack of neutrality for the settlement of disputes and the lack of strong protection against foreign enemies. Locke reasoned that while some governments might arise through sheer force, legitimate government required the consent of those governed. Government was therefore agreed upon by the people in the state of nature. Because the state of nature had no drastic problems, but was merely inconvenient, government was intended to preserve the positive aspects of life in the state of nature, including private property. However, property for Locke was not mere material possessions but also the life and liberty of subjects, which were God-given rights that they retained after the state of nature was perfected by civil government. But private property as material possessions was of paramount importance.

Locke asked how it was that humans came to own property, individually—before there was government—so that government would protect it. His answer was that although God had given "all the earth and its fruits" to mankind in common, He also commanded that they work. When someone mixed his labor with part of the great common, by hunting, gathering, or farming, he came to be the rightful owner of both that with which he mixed his labor and the rest of that entity. Moreover, this transformation through labor was transitive. The fruits of an employee's labor would belong to their employer. Locke wrote:

> Thus the grass my horse has bit; the turfs my servant has cut; and the ore I have digged in any place, where I have a right to them in common with others, become my property, without the assignation or consent of any body. The labour that was mine, removing them out of that common state they were in, hath fixed my property in them.

Twentieth-century philosopher Robert Nozick, in *Anarchy, State, and Utopia*, slyly asked about Locke's labor theory of ownership: "If I own a can of tomato juice and spill it in the sea so that its molecules (made radioactive, so I can check this) mingle evenly throughout the sea, do I thereby come to own the sea, or have I foolishly dissipated my tomato juice?" One could also ask, "If I work the surface of a piece of otherwise unowned land, how do I come to own its mineral and air rights?"

Locke approved of the use of precious objects as money, as a store of value to avoid waste, in the state of nature. His justification for the origin of private property has also been viewed as tied to his time, because it supported the enclosure movement, when lands historically used in common on village levels were appropriated for profit by wealthy large landowners. Throughout the *Second Treatise*, Locke claimed that labor, with a surplus convertible into money, was a motivation to develop "waste" land (i.e., land that had not been labored upon) and give it value. This labor–value argument could also be used to justify the seizure of land occupied by American indigenous people, some of whom did not work their land continuously, as the English and Europeans did, even though other tribes had permanent agricultural settlements. Locke thought that "the Indians in America" lacked the incentive to work their land, because they lacked money. This was not altogether correct. American tribes had *wampum* or useful objects that could be exchanged or kept as intrinsically valuable. What they lacked was fungible currency and strong desire to accumulate it. (Locke himself believed that money was ultimately entries in an abstract notational system and indigenous peoples also lacked that.)

The idea that private property has been earned has proved useful for later economic conceptions of democracy. However, many who labor all their lives own very little and those who own much may have never labored at all. Locke assumed that the fruits of labor by employees belong to their employers, a view that omits the rights of employees. Also, Locke's view that the value of land is wholly the result of how much labor has been expended on it leaves out the value of natural beauty, as well as human recreational needs for unspoiled environments. At our time, concerns about climate change emphasize the necessity for less land development, as well as less extraction of resources.

Locke was not a political radical and his prescriptions for government assumed ongoing peace and stability, along with prosperity for the industrious. But he also thought that while government could not survive if society were destroyed, society would endure if government were destroyed. Moreover, rebellion or revolution was justified, if a government or sovereign no longer represented the interests of the people, by violating their natural rights. Such action would return society to a state of nature that was also a state of war, because the ruler would be like a dangerous beast of prey who could be killed. He wrote:

> [W]henever the Legislators endeavour to take away, and destroy the Property of the People, or to reduce them to Slavery under Arbitrary Power, they put themselves into a state of War with the People, who are thereupon absolved from any farther Obedience, and are left to the common Refuge, which God hath provided for all

Men, against Force and Violence.... By this breach of Trust they forfeit the Power, the People had put into their hands, for quite contrary ends, and it devolves to the People, who have a Right to resume their original Liberty.

However, in Locke's historical context, it was not legislators who threatened the property of the people, but kings—Charles I and James II. Locke's *First Treatise of Government* was a protracted series of arguments, contra Robert Filmer's *Patriarcha* (1680), against the divine and absolute right of kings.

Rousseau's idea of the social contract balanced his original view of the nature of society with the role of government. Unlike Hobbes, Locke, and many others, Rousseau did not approach the subject of government from a political position or with specific political aims, and neither was he an academic scholar. Rather, he proceeded from morality and psychology. Nevertheless, his idea of the social contract was taken up by political totalitarians and radical liberals alike.

Rousseau was born in 1712 in Calvinist Geneva, a city state ruled by an influential minority of citizens. His mother died when he was nine days old and his father, a watchmaker in a long family tradition, brought him up with a great deal of reading, including Plutarch and sentimental fiction. His father left Geneva after a dispute and Rousseau himself left at age 16. Madame de Warens, his benefactress and mistress who was a Roman Catholic, oversaw his conversion to Catholicism and got him tutoring jobs.

Rousseau had broad interests, including development of a new notational system for music. He moved to Paris and met Thérèse Levasseur, a laundress with whom he had five children, all put up for adoption. Rousseau also became part of fashionable literary society and wrote for the pre-Revolutionary *Encyclopédie*. In 1750, he won an essay competition from the Academy of Dijon. The set subject was whether the arts and sciences had elevated or debased public morals. Rousseau's *Discourse on the Sciences and Arts* (*First Discourse*) won first prize. His arguments that science and art corrupted both individual and civic morality became the foundation for his social and political philosophy, as well as his moral psychology. And his creative life expanded. He wrote an opera, *The Village Soothsayer*, which was performed for more than 100 years. He also promoted Italian music because he extolled its melodies. His novels *Julie, ou La Nouvelle Héloise* and *Émile* followed his departure from Paris to a simpler way of life.

Émile was banned in Paris and Geneva, because it expressed views of religion that defied accepted orthodoxy. *The Social Contract*, published in 1762, was also banned in Geneva, where Rousseau had regained his citizenship after renouncing Catholicism. The philosopher David Hume rescued Rousseau from persecution from Genevan authorities and brought him to England. They fell out after about a year, due partly to Hume's overbearance and partly to Rousseau's paranoia. Rousseau began work on the *Confessions* at this time, and his *Dialogues* and *The Reveries of the Solitary Walker* followed. He died in 1778, probably of a stroke, although there were rumors of suicide. By that time, he was world famous. Many of Rousseau's readers considered him their personal friend and experienced great emotional catharsis while reading his novels; others strove to raise their children according to the principles by which Émile was educated. Rousseau was first buried on an island in a park in Ermenonville, but 16 years later, he was reburied in the Panthéon in Paris, as an icon of the French Revolution.

Themes and analyses developed in the *First Discourse*, *Émile*, *The Social Contract*, and *The Reveries of the Solitary Walker* portray natural humans as morally good in the state of nature, because they are solitary and isolated, without attachments, ambition, or even language. Rousseau agreed with Hobbes that competition, fear, and anxiety characterized human relations. But unlike Hobbes, he sought not only to quell such strife but rather identify its cause, so that it could be corrected. According to Rousseau, the cause of human ills was human relations. As a solitary being, man had *amour de soi*, or direct self-love; but as a social being, he was concerned with his reputation through *amour-propre*, or self-love based on the views of others. Individuals in society are motivated by *amour-propre* and dependence and manipulation plague all human social relations. Left alone, without society, the ideal, according to Rousseau, in both the natural state itself and reflection upon it, is what he called in *Reveries*, "the sweet sentiment of existence":

> In what does the enjoyment of such a situation consist? In nothing beyond ourselves, nothing foreign to our own existence, for while this state lasts (like the supreme) the enjoyment of that alone is sufficient felicity. The consciousness of existence, divested of every other sensation, is a sentiment of contentment and peace, which alone suffices to render it dear and satisfactory to whoever can put away those sensual and earthly affections which perpetually disturb and embitter our terrestrial felicity.

The fictional character Émile was brought up by a tutor who believed he was naturally morally good and took great care to control his relationships with those outside the household. Émile's happiness at being alive could thus be preserved. But Rousseau realized that most members of society were already psychologically and morally corrupt. His conception of democratic government provided a way to correct this condition through egalitarian benevolence, justice, and austere enforcement. A legislature of a select group of citizens would directly pass just laws and elect the executive. Both the laws and their application (by the executive) would express the *general will*, a collective desire for the good of everyone. Legal equality would eventually remove the differences supporting the corruptions of *amour-propre*, because the laws would apply to all citizens in the same way. There was to be a state religion and strict censorship. It was Rousseau's apparent indifference about which religion would be chosen by

the state that resulted in his condemnation by the Swiss
authorities.

Rousseau did not advocate a popular form of government, but one
designed to support the greatest amount of human freedom.
Underlying this freedom was a fundamental right not to be killed.
However, the social contract requires that each citizen be prepared
to give up their right not to be killed if the general will requires it:

> Now, the citizen is not a judge of the peril to which the law requires
> that he expose himself, and when the prince has said to him, "It is
> expedient for the State that you should die," he ought to die.

Comparisons

Hobbes, Locke, and Rousseau all posited conditions of human life
before or without government and for each their description of
that natural state or state of nature motivated their proposals for
specific kinds of government. Or, they may have begun with the
kind of government they were already committed to and then
"reverse engineered" it to describe a state of nature that would
justify it. Hobbes described humans as warlike and advocated
strong government to keep peace. Strong government expressed
the interests of his royalist patrons. Locke thought that humans
were naturally peaceable and advocated representative
government as a convenience to settle individual disputes and
organize protection from external enemies. Representative
government served the interests of his parliamentarian patron
and associates. Rousseau believed that government could correct
the corruption inflicted by society on naturally good human
beings. Rousseau was thinking morally, rather than politically,
although he had an abiding loyalty to Geneva, as well as a desire
to return, and his preferred form of government was modeled on
the existing structure of that Calvinist city.

It is interesting that both Hobbes, who thought that humans are naturally contentious, and Rousseau, who thought they were naturally peaceful, should propose totalitarian government. Their difference resulted from their views of society, as mirroring human nature according to Hobbes, but distorting it according to Rousseau. Hobbes therefore posited government strong enough to control human nature, whereas Rousseau posited government as an institution that would correct society. In contrast to both, Locke did not identify any intolerable problems with either human nature or society. This meant that there was no need for strong corrective government. Locke's views endured in liberal conceptions of democracy that minimized the role of government in human life. Hobbes produced a "law and order" conception of government that can still be invoked during emergencies, as states of exception. Apart from the totalitarian embrace of Rousseau's theory, his idea of government endures in progressive thought that since the 19th century has emphasized the role of government to create equality in society.

All three of these themes—the need for totalitarian government at times (Hobbes), the idea of minimal government to protect citizen interests as necessary (Locke), and the use of government for reform (Rousseau)—arose again and again as motivations for government formation, government reform, and government as a tool for solving problems in society. We will see them playing out in Chapters 5–8.

Chapter 5
Rights and revolutions: (exclusive) political equality

On the way to the guillotine in 1793, when Marie Antoinette was told that the people had no bread, she was reputed to reply, "Let them eat cake." But in his 1765 *Confessions*, Jean-Jacques Rousseau referred to a then-contemporary princess who may have been the original author of this insensitivity: "At length I recollected the thoughtless saying of a great princess, who, on being informed that the country people had no bread, replied, 'Then let them eat pastry!'" Marie Antoinette was only 9 years old in 1765, she did not become queen until 1774, and she went to the guillotine 19 years later.

The American and French revolutions are popularly celebrated as foundations for present day democracy. They did set up democratic government structures, but we would not call them democratic today, because they did not extend political rights to all of the people and their views of society did not include equality. The ideas and reality of rights that prevailed after both revolutions did not extend to women, slaves, or poor free men.

The ideologies of both revolutions relied on social contract theory: Locke for the Americans, Rousseau (at least in name) for the French, and, in a general way, Hobbesian insecurity as a motive for violent overthrow of government. The French Revolution was also Hobbesian in totalitarian control by whoever was in power at different stages. Specific directives for equal political rights or for equality in society had been absent in the writings of the social contract theorists and they were absent in the ideologies of these revolutions. Hobbes, Locke, and Rousseau did all believe that "the people" had ultimate political rights—the people could legitimately launch a revolution against a government that was not fulfilling its obligations to them. But they did not have broad or inclusive meanings of "the people." Also, they differed on the foundation for rights in general. According to Locke, rights were natural or God-given and endured after governments were formed, while for Hobbes and Rousseau, rights were created and protected by government.

The social contract theorists did not distinguish between the sovereign right of the people, who were already politically organized and could be represented by government officials or emergent leaders, and the direct right of people to participate in or influence their government. The framers of the US Constitutional Convention already had political standing as state delegates from the colonies, before they began the US Constitution with the words, "We the people." But in the French Revolution, there was less stability in the political organization of the people, so that numerous, changing political parties and clubs competed among themselves and came in and out of power. Emerging leaders such as the moderate Marquis de Lafayette, the radical Maximilien Robespierre, the military dictator Napoléon Bonaparte, and others with disparate views and aims claimed to speak for the people as they came to power. But they had not formally come to represent them, for instance through elections.

In comparing the American and French revolutions, there is also an important difference between a colony revolting against a parent country and the people revolting internally against their government. All of these differences, in foundations for political rights, the prior existence or absence of political organizations behind revolutionary leaders, and colonial versus internal revolution, resulted in different claims by leaders of the American and French revolutions, different revolutionary structures, and different kinds of democratic governments resulting from them. Each revolution also produced distinct ideologies.

The American Revolution

The American Revolution is mythically invoked as the radical founding of a democratic nation, with the ensuing constitution as its sacred blueprint. The revolution itself was justified by existing democratic principles and traditions that were already well established in Great Britain and respected throughout the colonies. English culture and economic investment were dominant in the colonies and were to persist through the 19th century. The revolution consisted of ideology, military action, and constitutions for both the states and the nation, which determined the structure and process of American government. The resulting conception of democracy emphasized the rights of privileged citizens under a democratic government, and those rights were based on British rights.

The American colonies had largely governed themselves after they were founded, with the approval of the British monarchy, but they had no formal representation in the British parliament that officially governed them. The colonies had to pay taxes to Britain but had no say in how that money was spent. They could buy only British goods, under a monopoly on trade, but could not in turn sell their goods to the mother country. The Stamp Act of 1765 levied a colonial tax on publications and when colonists protested, they stood on their rights as Englishmen. Patrick Henry proclaimed in the Virginia Stamp Act Resolutions of 1765:

> Resolved, that by two royal charters, granted by King James I, the colonists aforesaid are declared entitled to all liberties, privileges, and immunities of denizens and natural subjects to all intents and

purposes as if they had been abiding and born within the Realm of England.

John Adams went deeper, writing, "The rights of Englishmen are derived from God, not from king or Parliament, and would be secured by the study of history, law, and tradition."

The Stamp Act was repealed but further resistance was sparked by the Townshend Acts of 1767. The Townshend Acts suspended colonial assemblies, imposed new duties on imported goods, gave the East India Tea Company special status for imports, and allowed for the quartering of British troops. British troops were sent to Boston, resulting in the Boston Massacre of 1770, followed by colonials burning the *Gaspee* in 1772 and the Boston Tea Party in 1773. The British then closed Boston Harbor and shut down self-government by the Massachusetts Bay Colony. In 1774, the Patriots began to organize colonial forces at the Continental Congress.

The American colonial governments each transferred their power to a state Provincial Congress and the national Continental Congress asserted the rights of its members as Englishmen against George III. Independence was declared on July 2, 1776. The Continental Army led by George Washington retook Boston and captured a British army at Saratoga. France joined as an ally and was active from 1778 on. The combination of the Continental Army and French troops was victorious at Yorktown in 1781 and the Treaty of Paris was signed in 1783. The Articles of Confederation shaped the national government until the Philadelphia Convention produced the United States Constitution, which was ratified by the states in 1788 (Figure 5).

The United States Constitution set up a federal form of government with delineated powers over war and peace and interstate commerce for the national government. The powers of

5. 1788: The inauguration of George Washington as the first President of the United States. Also present are (from left) Alexander Hamilton, Robert R. Livingston, Roger Sherman, Mr Otis, Vice President John Adams, Baron Von Steuben, and General Henry Knox. Original Artwork: Printed by Currier & Ives.

this national government were separated among a president, a bicameral legislature, and a national judiciary. Residual powers concerning the regulation of ordinary life, including voting and criminal law, were left to the states. The first 10 amendments to the US Constitution granted basic individual rights, to free speech, assembly, and press, freedom from government interference in religion, due process in legal proceedings, and protection of private property from arbitrary government seizure. Although the US national government had a strained and disorganized budget at the outset, the practical result was the establishment of the first national liberal democratic government in the West, and, so far, the longest-lasting one.

The establishment of the US government built on the ideology of the American Revolution, a history of British rights, and colonial political structures. American revolutionary ideology had stressed both collective and individual rights, with emphasis on the words "equality" and "liberty." Equality was tied to the stated English rights of colonists. Liberty often meant political freedom from taxation without representation and the absence of external military force or occupation. The social contract principle that those governed had to consent to their government had been invoked against British control of affairs in the American colonies, but within the new United States, suffrage required some degree of property ownership. After the Declaration of Independence, many of the states had constructed their own constitutions and these contributed to the elements of the US Constitution. The deliberate and methodical construction of the US Constitution by state representatives constituted federal consent to the national government.

As in the revolutionary period in England from the 1640s to 1689 (see Chapter 4), those who led the American Revolution wanted equality with those of greater wealth and power. They had British lords and nobles in mind, because equality did not flow down from the relatively privileged positions of revolutionary leaders. But Americans were to have no hereditary ranks, titles, or public offices. Black chattel slavery continued, and slaves counted for 3/5 of a person in political representation; Native American property was appropriated and reapportioned by the Paris treaty, without their consent; women could not vote. These exclusions contrasted with support for the revolution that had been provided militarily by tens of thousands of African Americans and Native Americans. The medical and domestic contributions of women, who either managed at home on their own or directly participated in the war, were ignored. And neither was male suffrage universal, although all classes had participated in the war. Indeed, before serving as the first vice president and second president, John Adams had explicitly opposed more broad suffrage. On May 26, 1776, writing to his friend James Sullivan, a member of the Massachusetts General Court, he concluded:

Depend upon it, sir, it is dangerous to open So fruitful a Source of Controversy and Altercation, as would be opened by attempting to alter the Qualifications of Voters. There will be no End of it. New Claims will arise. Women will demand a Vote. Lads from 12 to 21 will think their Rights not enough attended to, and every Man, who has not a Farthing, will demand an equal Voice with any other in all Acts of State. It tends to confound and destroy all Distinctions, and prostrate all Ranks, to one common Levell.

In the new state constitutions of Maryland, Virginia, Delaware, New York, and Massachusetts, property ownership was required for voting. New Jersey and New Hampshire had low property requirements; Pennsylvania had none until they were instituted in 1790.

The French Revolution

The French Revolution from 1789 to 1799 was a chaotic and violent process that did not settle into peaceful, organized, and regulative government until it was well over. It upended the social order in France and imposed great suffering throughout France and abroad. European countries were drawn into related wars, until the French Consulate came to power.

The French Revolution began with social protest and rioting in reaction to high unemployment and increased food prices due to poor harvests. In response, for the first time since 1614, in May 1789, King Louis XVI convened the Estates General. By June, after the Estates had restructured itself as the National Assembly, feudalism and slavery were abolished, and the government took control of the Catholic Church and its property. Suffrage was expanded, but only to include tax-paying men over age 25, who were about 15 percent of the population—their yearly taxes had to be equal to three days of labor wages at local rates. They were the active citizens who could elect the members of the National Assembly.

The June reforms did not quell social turmoil, especially when Louis XVI planned to move the National Assembly away from Paris. The Bastille was a medieval fortress built to guard Paris from the east which had become a state prison for high-level detainees. Its walls were 100 feet high, behind a moat, and it was guarded by 80 soldiers and 30 Swiss mercenaries. Bernard-René Jourdan de Launay, the military governor of the Bastille, anticipated an attack and was given an additional 250 barrels of gunpowder and reinforcements on July 12, 1789. He raised the drawbridges. On July 14, a growing crowd with muskets, swords, and other weapons gathered. Launay surrendered but was killed by a mob before he could be arrested and arraigned, and his head was paraded on a pike. There were only seven prisoners to be freed—four forgers, a sex offender, and two "lunatics." But the symbolism was powerful, and Bastille Day is still celebrated in France.

Constitutional reforms resulted in the First French Republic in 1792. Although he had agreed to legal limits on the monarchy, King Louis XVI was executed the next year, under a faction of the Girondins. The Committee of Public Safety, headed by Maximilien Robespierre, came into power under a radical Jacobin faction to begin a Reign of Terror that lasted about a year. Almost 17,000 were executed in Paris and tens of thousands more throughout France. Marie Antoinette was guillotined, as was Robespierre himself. Real and suspected counter-revolutionary activities and persons were brutally dealt with, and food shortages extended the suffering of the poor and their ongoing protests and riots. Overall, government was conducted under a state of emergency that was presented as temporary, until the Republic was *pure et dure* (pure and strong). The leaders of the revolution proclaimed it to be the ongoing creation of democracy. They were put forth by existing political groups already in power, rather than through institutional processes such as voting, and their rise was acknowledged by acclaim.

French ideologues proselytized and the spirit of "liberty, equality, fraternity" was akin to a religious movement, inspiring revolts against arbitrary rule in other parts of the world. The slave revolt in Haiti from 1791 to 1804 was a direct result of the revolutionary ideology that began in France. This conflict between Haitian slaves and the French and British military who tried to protect the colonists resulted in Haitian independence from France. France had first abolished slavery, although by the end of the Haitian revolt, slavery had been reinstated.

Military victories brought prestige to the revolutionary government and were believed to unite France. France had declared war against Austria in 1792 and then invaded and annexed the Austrian Netherlands. By 1793, France declared war on Spain and Britain. National boundaries were redrawn, and, in the United States, President Thomas Jefferson negotiated the Louisiana Purchase with Napoléon in 1803.

Napoléon Buonaparte could rely on mass conscription for his fighting forces, because he was so popular. He rose to power through his military leadership during the Revolutionary Wars, making himself emperor of the French from 1804 to 1814 and again in 1815. The Napoleonic Code, modelled on Roman law, was approved for France in 1804, after a Commission met 80 times. Although the planning and discussion of the Code were democratic, its content was exclusive: only male citizens had equal rights, including the right to religious dissent; women did not have individual rights; slavery remained. Law was divided into commercial and criminal branches, with civil law over property and the family. The Code applied to all colonies and territories and influenced other European nations and South America.

The culture of the French Revolution, including the Reign of Terror, fascinated many. "Citoyen" (Citizen) became the new egalitarian title and universal form of address. The guillotine had been invented as a medical device for efficient executions, but because the fall of the blade was always the same, it became a symbol of equality. "La Marseillaise" became an enduring song of revolution, to be taken up in the Russian Revolution of 1917.

The ideology of the French Revolution was not limited to the rights of French people but was meant to encompass all humankind. This was evident in *The Declaration of the Rights of Man and of the Citizen*, written by the Marquis de Lafayette with Thomas Jefferson and issued by the French National Constituent Assembly in 1789. Lafayette had been in command during the American Revolution when Yorktown was decisively seized. Radical for its time, *The Declaration* was first included in the beginning of the French constitutions of the Fourth and Fifth French Republics (1946 and 1958) and continued to be constitutional in France; in 2003, it was listed on UNESCO's Memory of the World register. The 17 articles of this Declaration were plainly and succinctly set forth. Some were based on the historical precedents of the Magna Carta and the US Declaration of Independence and the US Constitution, but others introduced new abstractions. Articles I–V proclaimed rights against governments, rejecting absolute rule apart from the will of the people of a nation. Article VI presented the idea of the general will, as Rousseau had introduced it in his *Social Contract*, although it had no concrete legal implementation. Thus:

> VI. Law is the expression of the general will. All citizens have the right to take part personally, or by their representatives, in its formation. It must be the same for all, whether it protects or punishes. All citizens, being equal in its eyes, are equally eligible to all public dignities, places, and employments, according to their capacities, and without other distinction than that of their virtues and talents.

The rights asserted in VIII–XVII of the Declaration had been stated in the Magna Carta and the US Declaration of Independence, but here they were proclaimed as universal rights.

The requirements for a constitution consisting of the guarantee of natural rights and a division of powers in government were proclaimed for all societies in Article XVI:

> Any society in which the guarantee of the rights is not secured, or the separation of powers not determined, has no constitution at all.

Private property was held to be sacred, here more in keeping with Locke than Rousseau:

> XVII. Property being a sacred and inviolable right, no one can be deprived of it, unless legally established public necessity evidently demands it, under the condition of a just and prior indemnity.

Critiques of the revolutions

Several critical reactions to both the American and French revolutions are important for more modern discussions of democracy. Key elements of this criticism include: English cultural dominance in the American revolutionary period and beyond; Alexis de Tocqueville's consideration of American federalism; Friedrich von Gentz's unfavorable view of the French Revolution compared to the American Revolution; and criticism of the French Revolution by Edmund Burke.

While the United States as an independent nation was no longer a British colony, its British parentage endured culturally and economically. In 1790, English Americans were almost half of the population and the largest nationality. Many English Americans were wealthy before the revolution and as the new country expanded they grew wealthier by buying land, controlling trade, and holding public office. The Immigration and Naturalization Act of 1790 restricted naturalization to "free white persons" of "good moral character." This meant that indentured servants, slaves, free blacks, and Native Americans could not be citizens; and in 1795, a five-year residence requirement was added to citizenship eligibility. In Massachusetts, the English Puritans had imposed modesty, restraint in entertainment, and "blue laws" that restricted recreational activities and the sale of hard goods and consumables on Sundays, when alcohol sales were also banned. English was the common language throughout the colonies, and households were based on nuclear families, as they were in England. Protestantism, consisting mainly of dissenters from the Anglican Church of England, such as Baptists, Methodists, Quakers, and Puritans (and dissenters against them), was the dominant religion. Members of other groups had to assimilate to English Protestant culture before joining the establishment.

The colonies had imported British finished goods that set the style of daily life. From parlors to poor houses, colonists drank English tea from porcelain cups. There was a credit system to support consumer purchases of English clothing and interior décor. This commerce was only interrupted by the Revolutionary War. Afterwards, England was not only a major supplier for mass consumption but provided most of the foreign investment in land, industrial development, railroads, mining, and cattle ranching. The War of 1812 was another interruption that did not curtail Anglo cultural and economic dominance. The importance of English culture in the United States made it easy to import and continue undemocratic inequalities that may not have been fully examined until the 20th century, where they persisted in racial and gender inequality and discrimination against non-Anglo immigrants.

Statesman and political theorist Alexis de Tocqueville (1805–59) sought to convince the European aristocratic classes that democracy was the political trend of the future in his two-volume *Democracy in America* (1835–40) and his major work *L'Ancien Régime et la Révolution/The Old Regime and the Revolution* (1856). Many Tories (English royalist sympathizers) were critical of the new federal government structure of the United States and predicted eventual anarchy, because the states had so much power. But de Tocqueville was skeptical of the role of central government in democracy.

De Tocqueville was concerned that the American national government would simply preside over a mass of individuals who were more interested in private consumption and pleasures than the kind of civic participation necessary to protect their freedoms. He thought that majority rule would crush dissenting individuality. However, he was optimistic that local organizational structures, including civic, business, and cultural groups, would draw Americans into civic participation that would fill the gap between a powerful central government and isolated individuals. He may have overlooked the important role of American state governments for regulating daily life. De Tocqueville also believed that the American ability to connect the absence of a state religion to their own religious freedom would support enthusiastic protection of other individual freedoms. He could not have foreseen the splintering effect of 21st-century social media, nor the rise of political religious intolerance in ongoing abortion and immigration debates.

The American Revolution was justified by reference to existing law and the constitution founded the United States government with divisions of power and rights reserved for citizens. Political writer and diplomat Friedrich von Gentz (1764–1842) favorably compared it to the French Revolution. Gentz pointed to the French revolutionary use of fictive rights and arbitrary popular will to create unjustified violent repression and international war, as well as regicide, without coherent or consistent constitutional foundation. Gentz's comparison may falter, however, given the acceptance of slavery in the US Constitution. Also, if rights are limited to actual law, the concept of human rights as a moral imperative, apart from government, is ruled out. Genz could not have anticipated how societal tensions concerning racial identities and status could come to dominate politics.

Others viewed the French Revolution as a threat to values and tradition that were necessary for future progress, as well as stability. Edmund Burke (1729–97) was an Irish political theorist and member of the British House of Commons before the American Revolutionary War. As a parliamentarian, Burke was sympathetic to American rights against external taxation, and he tried to reconcile them with British sovereignty over an empire. Burke founded modern political conservatism in his 1790 *Reflections on the Revolution in France*. He broadly criticized revolution itself as a political method, writing: "A spirit of innovation is generally the result of a selfish temper and confined views. People will not look forward to posterity, who never look backward to their ancestors." Burke argued that liberty was not the only political value, because the power of the people as sovereign also required restraint. It was important for progress that the people be ruled by ideas to avoid government by brute force in place of the "effective command of opinion." Informed opinion required knowledge of the history of justice and the patterns of social relations that held it in place. Burke took what we would call "propaganda" easily in stride, because he assumed that conservative propaganda was necessary to preserve the high value of tradition.

A note on rights

The conception of democracy shared by the American and French revolutions asserted the rights of citizens and the obligation of government to protect them, under law, and by force if necessary. However, neither revolution itself, nor criticism of the period, settled the question of the nature of such rights. The rights claimed in the American Revolution were reasserted English rights and the leaders of the French Revolution simply proclaimed universal political rights. Rights already protected by government are *positive rights*, and rights simply proclaimed could be based on religion, human nature, or intuition, so that claims that they are universal could seem "abstract" or "fictive."

The idea of English rights was usually taken to refer to common law and tradition. But to expand who actually had such lawful rights, further recourse beyond positive law was necessary. For example, during the English Civil War, there had been calls to expand existing suffrage beyond property owners. Colonel Thomas Rainsborough (1610–48) of the New Model Army asserted, "The poorest he that is in England has life to live as the greatest he." Rainsborough's claim seemed to rest on *nativism*, a deeper form of English nationalism used to expand English rights that already existed. (But, of course, nativism has not been limited to England and has been used to restrict rights of non-natives in other contexts.) Rainsborough's claim was not successful. Instead, the argument prevailed that an expansion of suffrage would override existing property ownership. The property-owning rationale rested partly on beliefs dating to antiquity that citizens should be informed and educated and that only those who owned property had the leisure to attain that, and partly on persistent racism and sexism. Property ownership as a requirement for suffrage continued in England and later in the United States until the presidential election of 1828, when all white males could vote in most states. Suffrage restrictions against both African Americans and women continued until the Civil War amendments to the US Constitution, the 19th Amendment granting women the right to vote in 1920, and the Civil Rights legislation of the mid-1960s.

The revolutionary period sparked political discussion among an expanded, educated public of readers and writers focused on universal voting rights, the position of women in civil society, and the abolition of slavery. These issues, together with the plight of the poor, became the new issues of modernity. Limitations on suffrage led some political thinkers to believe that the reliance on rights and government alone was insufficient to secure equality. Nineteenth-century progressives were to take another approach by focusing on those inequalities in society that limited citizenship rights. Unlike Burke, they were to focus on tradition to change it.

Chapter 6
Social progressivism: toward democracy in society

Many who live in modern democracies now take it for granted that government agencies exist that have the power and authority to intervene against child abuse. But this function of government is relatively recent. In 1874, Mary Ellen Wilson had been beaten, cut, burned, and confined to an apartment in New York City for seven years. Henry Bergh of the ASPCA (American Society for the Prevention of Cruelty to Animals) helped rescue her and the ASPCA used its authority to charter the NYSPCC (New York Society for the Prevention of Cruelty to Children). In the United States, there were laws against cruelty to animals before child abuse was legally addressed. In the UK, the order of legislation was reversed. In 1889, in response to Queen Victoria's advocacy, parliament passed the extensive Prevention of Cruelty to, and Protection of, Children Act, which aimed to end the neglect and abuse of children, as well as exploitation of their labor. In England and Wales, the anti-cruelty Protection of Animals Act was passed in 1911. But in both the US and UK, legislation was preceded by local and national societies for the prevention of cruelty to both children and animals. At this time, such anti-cruelty legislation, as well as societies, extends throughout the developed democratic world.

The case of Mary Ellen Wilson is an example of child welfare laws, a correction of one of many inequalities and injustices within society, which democratic government can now address and regulate. (Included are commerce, business practices and certification, and employment safety, just to name a few.) Such regulations ensure that society itself is democratic, so that those uninformed or vulnerable are not exploited, fooled, injured, or killed. There are many conceptions of democratic society, from complete safety-net coverage to maximally unrestrained individual liberties. Generally, democratic society is supposed to be humane. However, democratic society has not automatically been associated with democratic government. Moral intuitions and principles have been necessary to democratize society, through government outreach into it. That humane role of government required an extension in ideas of democracy from a focus on the nature of government structure and procedure to the role of government in making society itself more just.

In the ancient, medieval, and Renaissance worlds, conceptions and practices of democracy pertained to the structure and process of government. Those already advantaged or privileged in society were able to join the political ruling group or have their interests represented within it. And those societally disadvantaged or low in status were left out. The great modern revolutions that led to more democratic forms of government, in Britain, the United States, and France, followed the same pattern. But the political ideology of the French Revolution also introduced general ideas of universal human rights, which in principle extended to those politically excluded, although at that time, only as an abstract principle. Compassion for the poor and ideas of human equality date back to ancient stoicism and cosmopolitanism and were emphasized in major religions, especially Christianity. However, it took a long time for such moral thoughts and feelings to be expressed by governments. That is, neither democratic governmental structures, nor abstract universal claims, nor religious compassion, directly alleviated exploitation of the poor, the lack of rights for women, and chattel slavery. To address such societal inequality, what was needed was a shift in attention from how people were ruled under democratic government and laws, to how people lived. The question of who could get political power, either directly, or through advocates, becomes the question of who *should* get political power. That was, and still is, a moral question.

In the ancient world, moral issues were centered on character, how privileged individuals could become their own best selves, through right reasoning and action. Christianity introduced altruism into human relations, but even when the Catholic Church had ultimate power, members of the flock were treated as religious, rather than political, subjects. Spiritual reward in heaven after death was not universal but restricted to Christians. And while charity was supported, Christian altruism did not oppose the societal inequalities that made it necessary.

To answer questions of who should get political power, the social order required examination from a practical moral perspective. And then, for an answer or answers to become reality, there had to be argument, advocacy, and sometimes organized social movements that would result in creating new political power, changes in laws, and even new laws. Changes in government policies would also be needed to implement legal changes, because legal changes would have to be applied and obeyed. The general aim would be egalitarian society, under democratic government, a combination of ideas and action that was the beginning of *political progressivism*.

Political progressivism rests on the belief that law and government can improve human well-being. It is related to a more general view that history itself brings progress, a view that flourished in the 19th century, although its initial focus was not on societal inequalities. Thinkers in earlier centuries, going back to Plato and Aristotle, had viewed human history in terms of cycles, entailing that even the best forms of government and society would eventually decline. The progressive view has been not only that human well-being can and should improve, but that it does improve, through human activity over time. Nineteenth-century progressive thinkers variably posited the causes of progress as growth in knowledge, particularly in the physical sciences, increases in production, or naturally benevolent human nature. Measures of human well-being were not precise, but examples could include broad improvements in literacy through the expansion of education and the betterment of public health from the identification of bacterial pathogens that cause infectious disease. Child labor was restricted in European countries during the 19th century, but not in the United States until the 1930s. Child labor remains a global problem in the early 21st century.

The first part of this chapter is a brief discussion of ideas of progress. The second part will focus on political theorists who sought to make society more egalitarian, for moral reasons— Jeremy Bentham, John Stuart Mill, and Karl Marx. The third part is a brief discussion of social and political reform movements in 19th-century America. The chapter concludes with reflections on social progressivism and history.

Theories of progress

Theories of progress began with modernity. Thomas Hobbes believed that the chief social goods of human life, primarily security, but also art, science, and commerce, were only possible under strong government to which those governed had originally consented. Most political theorists in the Western tradition assumed that even without consent, human life was better with government than without it, so that the institution of human government was itself a mark of human progress. Scottish Enlightenment philosopher David Hume (1711–76) claimed, in *Of the Rise and Progress of the Arts and Sciences* (1748), that progress in art and science required political security. Hume thought that a republic furthered this advancement because its free public could voice its appreciation of technological innovations.

However, not all theories of progress relied on an important role for government. For instance, Hume's friend, Scottish economist and philosopher Adam Smith (1723–90), put his faith in the marketplace. Smith posited an "invisible hand," whereby the individual pursuit of economic self-interest, together with division of labor, resulted in greater prosperity for all. Smith's *The Wealth of Nations*, published in 1776, became a classic modern justification for capitalism with minimal government intervention.

Smith had a holistic view of progress that applied to the entire nation. By contrast, moral views about egalitarian progress within nations focused on specific groups and conditions within nations. Since the European Enlightenment (from the late 1600s to 1815) holistic progressivism has not included concerns about equality within society. To this day, neoliberals accept great inequalities of wealth within nations, provided that national productivity is on the upswing. Progress has also been measured and projected based on brilliant achievements in the arts, philosophy, and science. For instance, Marie Jean Caritat, Marquis de Condorcet (1743–94) expressed the French Enlightenment enthusiasm for empirical science as a progressive force. Condorcet was in prison in 1795, during the Reign of Terror, when he wrote *Outlines of an Historical View of the Progress of the Human Mind*. That his personal troubles did not dampen his optimism suggests that those who hold ideas of holistic progress may be inured to their own misery, as well as that of others.

Some thinkers considered progress in terms of war and peace. German philosopher Immanuel Kant (1724–1804) believed that humanity was progressing toward world peace. In *Ideas toward a Universal History with a Cosmopolitan Purpose* (1784), he reasoned that human beings cannot develop their faculties in individual lifetimes, but that the human race as a whole will develop all human faculties over time. This will require freedom and peace, to enable cooperation and the creation of relevant institutions in society. Because humans share "unsocial sociability," cooperation is contentious, leading to a need for political organizations that could become republics. In *Perpetual Peace* (1795), Kant defined a republic as a state with free and equal citizens under law. Such citizens would be adverse to the cost of war and federations of republics could thereby exist in perpetual peace.

German philosopher G. W. F. Hegel (1770–1831) took Kant's idea of unsocial sociability further, into the positive uses of war. In *Elements of the Philosophy of Right* (1821), he posited the progress of the world as realization and expression of its Spirit (*Geist*), in nation states. The resolution of ideological conflict, and the rise and fall of "world-historical" leaders, also fueled progress. Both Kant and Hegel were willing to accept human suffering on the path toward progress of the whole. In *Ideas toward a Universal History with a Cosmopolitan Purpose*, Kant had referred to the "glittering misery" of parts of humanity (7th thesis).

Progressive ideas for society

Enlightenment ideas of progress as connected to democratic government sparked specific attention to egalitarian progress in society. It is this commitment to progress toward equality in society that deserves the name "progressivism." Jeremy Bentham and John Stuart Mill approached progress with the moral goal of the greatest pleasure or happiness for the greatest number. Karl Marx and Friedrich Engels called for the revolutionary unity of workers under capitalism, as both morally imperative and historically inevitable. All were political progressives who were motivated by moral intuitions and principles.

English philosopher and jurist Jeremy Bentham (1748–1832) drew a bright line between abstract rights and egalitarian changes in society. In his 1789 *Anarchical Follies*, Bentham criticized the French "Declaration of the Rights of Man and the Citizen," claiming that the idea of natural rights was "nonsense on stilts." According to Bentham, there could not be any rights outside of government and the very idea of such rights was invented to overthrow laws, with the end result of anarchy. In his *An Introduction to the Principles of Morals and Legislation* (1789), Bentham proposed strong, detailed principles for the reform of British society, without reliance on ideas of rights. He reasoned from the moral theory of utilitarianism that advocated the greatest good—more pleasure and/or less pain—for the greatest number. And his applications of utilitarianism were very specific.

Bentham sought to reform both corrupt laws and cruel social practices in the penal system. In *Panopticon Letters* (1787), he presented a new design for a prison that was to have spiraling architecture, so that every inmate could be constantly observed. This architecture would make it possible to reform both the behavior and thoughts of prisoners. Bentham meticulously planned for financing the institution with the proceeds from prisoners' labor and even offered his own services as its "governor." He proposed the *panopticon* over decades but could never get it funded. Bentham also had plans for codifying all of the laws of England and the states of the United States in a grand design he called a *Pannomion*, but neither was that taken up. Bentham bequeathed his body to be dissected and preserved for educational viewing as an "auto-icon"; it is still on view in a glass case at University College London, with his head kept elsewhere. The panopticon, pannomion, and auto-icon may make Bentham look like a crackpot, but there was much more to him than that.

Bentham also advocated the abolition of slavery, abolition of the death penalty, and reform of laws against homosexuality. He supported the full emancipation of women, as well as their suffrage and equality with men as legislators. He was also a strong advocate for minimizing animal suffering, writing in *Principles of Morals and Legislation*: "The question is not, Can they reason?

nor Can they talk? but, Can they suffer? Why should the law refuse its protection to any sensitive being?"

Bentham's support of what remain progressive causes—prison reform, animal rights, acceptance of LGBTQ+ people, women's full emancipation—only seems to be politically democratic in focusing on the well-being of those governed. But his reform ideas were based on his broader moral principle that pain is intrinsically bad and pleasure intrinsically good. The ultimate aim of everyone should be the greatest happiness for the greatest number. Bentham did not distinguish between emotional happiness and physical pleasure, and in *The Rationale of Reward* (1825) he asserted, "Prejudice apart, the game of push-pin [a child's game of dueling pins] is of equal value with the arts and sciences of music and poetry."

All rules and actions, especially those of leaders and officials, could be quantitatively assessed and compared in the Benthamite calculus (also known as the "Felicific Calculus"). A resulting pleasure or pain could be measured as something to be sought or avoided in terms of its *vectors*: Intensity—how strong is it? Duration—how long will it last? Certainty—how likely is it to occur? Proximity—how close is it? Fecundity—will it produce more pains or pleasure like itself? Purity—is it alloyed with its opposite? And Extent—how many will be affected? The calculated extent of a pleasure or pain was particularly important because each person was to count for one, and no one more than one.

Because Bentham's utilitarianism has seemed to be democratic in seeking to promote the greater good, social reformers who shared that goal have often also shared Bentham's moral foundation of utilitarianism. It makes sense that as many should be free of life's ills as possible. But John Stuart Mill (1806–73), although raised according to utilitarian principles (his father, James, was a close friend of Jeremy Bentham), was more interested in democratic government than Bentham and his approach to utilitarianism was more critical. Mill favored democratic representative government and the difference between push-pin and poetry mattered for him. He shared Bentham's advocacy of freedom of expression and women's emancipation but delved into each more philosophically.

Mill called representative government "the ideal kind of a perfect government," although he was less interested in who was represented than in the importance of discussion and debate among lawmakers. Mill agreed with Bentham that the "sinister interest of the few" could be countered by universal suffrage, regular elections, and secret ballots. And, following Bentham, he based these democratic ideas on the greatest good for the greatest number, rather than natural rights. But Mill did not believe that a mere democratic election carried by a majority entailed that the right decisions would be made. Instead, he proposed rule by knowledgeable persons, the "instructed few."

In *Considerations on Representative Government* (1861), Mill argued that a single class should dominate a democratically elected legislature. He advocated a Commission of Legislation to propose laws to an assembly elected by the majority. This was to be "the pure idea of democracy," because inclusion of the instructed few was as important as the will of the "mere majority." Thus, Mill wrote in chapter XIX of *Considerations*:

> The national institutions should place all things that they are concerned with before the mind of the citizen in the light in which it is for his good that he should regard them: and as it is for his good that he should think that every one is entitled to some influence, but the better and wiser to more than others.

Mill's idea of popular election of ultimate lawmakers dated back to the French Revolution, Jean-Jacques Rousseau's *Social Contract*, and before then, Roman republicanism. And, like his political predecessors, Mill advocated an educated electorate. Even before he considered the structure of government, Mill had developed his distrust of majority rule. In *On Liberty* (1859), he supported an open society in which different lifestyles and "experiments in living" could be freely expressed. Within society, minorities—and here Mill referred to smaller numbers of elite and progressive people rather than racial and ethnic disadvantaged groups, which "minorities" means today—ought to be protected from majorities. (He was here inspired by Alexis de Tocqueville's concerns that democratic government by majority rule would stifle minority dissent.) Mill recognized that freedom of speech should be broader than freedom of action, because he viewed speech as a vital intellectual activity that has less harmful potential than action. Speech had to be exercised, so that those whose views were rational and correct would be willing to constantly defend them. He wrote in chapter II of *On Liberty*:

> Even if the received opinion be not only true, but the whole truth; unless it is suffered to be, and actually is, vigorously and earnestly contested, it will, by most of those who receive it, be held in the manner of a prejudice, with little comprehension or feeling of its rational grounds.

Mill did not focus on whether all people had a political right to political participation or personal freedom. Instead, his goal was the moral utilitarian aim for more happiness in the long run. This was not mere pleasure in Bentham's sense, but happiness based on "higher pleasures." Push-pin was not as good as poetry. For Mill, "pleasure" often referred to what he called "lower pleasures" or short-term enjoyments that were mostly physical. He thought that the higher pleasures of friendship, literature, poetry, and other forms of delayed gratification were better. His authority for that was the judgment of those who had experienced both kinds of pleasure.

Mill has understandably been accused of elitism. His emphasis on higher pleasures matches his preference for rule by an informed few. Not everyone has the education and social connections to join a political elite, and many may not have the leisure to cultivate higher pleasures. As a result, Mill's conception of social reform is not fully democratic, because it does not take everyone into account. But Mill's personal experience was rarefied. Based on the utilitarian principles developed by Bentham and his father, he was raised to become a leader of his generation of radicals. He learned Greek at age 3, Latin at 8, and knew the classical canon by 12. This was followed by political philosophy, logic, economics, and metaphysics, with science as a hobby. He grew depressed in his early 20s and turned to Romantic poetry and literature. His liberal education was supported by Harriet Taylor, with whom he fell in love in 1831. Taylor was married and their relationship was platonic until her husband died. After they married in 1851, Taylor continued to inspire Mill and they worked closely together. Her influence on *On Liberty* and *The Subjection of Women* is now widely recognized. When he was elected MP for the city of Westminster in 1865, his platform included women's suffrage.

Mill's arguments for women's emancipation resembled Mary Wollstonecraft's in her *Vindication of the Rights of Women* (1792). Educated women would be better wives and mothers and emancipated women would contribute to the economic and political life of the nation. However, where Wollstonecraft based her advocacy on women's God-given rights as rational beings, Mill stressed their numbers as half of the human race. If women were emancipated, their contributions would have substantial effects on the happiness of men, as well as their own. Mill had a much greater influence on the success of women's causes than Wollstonecraft, because he was the most famous 19th-century (male) philosopher.

Karl Marx and Friedrich Engels

German philosopher, activist, and scholar Karl Marx (1818–83) followed Hegel by thinking in world progressive political terms. But unlike Hegel, Marx was a practical thinker, not interested in the expression of *Geist* (abstract spirit), but in real economic and social conditions within European society. As he put it in the 11th of his *Theses on Feuerbach* (1845), "philosophers have only interpreted the world in various ways, the point is to change it." Marx worked neither in the tradition of human rights, nor within the framework of democratic government, because he did not think that those without political power could get it in existing democracies that favored property owners.

Marx's radical publications resulted in exile from France and Germany, and from 1849 he lived in London with his family. He earned sporadic money from his writings (including hundreds of articles for the *New York Herald Tribune*), but he was mainly supported by his friend and collaborator Friedrich Engels (1820–95), whose father owned textile factories in England and Germany. Marx and his wife Jenny von Westphalen, a former aristocrat, endured poverty and ill-health. Jenny lost her hearing and was disfigured by smallpox, and both had liver ailments. At times Jenny had to pawn his pants to buy provisions. Marx also suffered from persistent boils (which he wrote to Engels were "truly proletarian"). Jenny was also active in political organizing, and she helped Marx in his writing. They had seven children. In his will, Engels provided for the two daughters who survived.

Marx had met Engels in 1844 and was convinced by his thesis in "The Condition of the Working Class in England" that the working class would drive the ultimate historical revolution. In 1848, Marx and Engels co-authored "The Communist Manifesto," which they presented as an action plan for the Communist League. It began, "The history of all hitherto existing society is the history of class struggles." Marx's main criticism of capitalism was summarized through a world historical account of production in human societies. The main idea was to champion the Communist League's international political party as the vanguard for continuing workers' revolutions. Marx was accused of donating money to revolutions in France and Belgium; he supported revolutionary activities in French Algeria, Ireland, and India. But he was skeptical that communism could succeed in Russia, because of its authoritarian government that aspired to world domination.

Marx's vision of what would happen after revolution was vaguely utopian. His work is associated with the phrase "the dictatorship of the proletariat," a transitional period until the state "withered away." Marx believed that politics were the result of economic arrangements, and that the bourgeoisie or dominant class under capitalism would have to be overthrown for the proletariat or working class to realize its goals. This was both an aspirational view and a call for revolutionary action. It was also a grand historical prediction, based on his interpretation of history as driven by the economics of societally dominant forms of production. Marx did not explicitly claim that the capitalist treatment of workers was unjust. His idea of historical necessity did the work of "justification" for revolution—the workers' revolution was historically determined. Capitalists were caught up in the competitive pressures in free markets that created a constant need to take risks and expand business. Revolution would occur as a result of the cycle of expansion and contraction within capitalism—boom and bust—which at the right time would make the situation of workers intolerable to them. This intolerability would motivate them to organize and assert their interests by violently seizing control of the means of production. The obvious question here is why, if workers' revolution is historically determined, does it need to be egged on?

In his 1859 "A Contribution to the Critique of Political Economy," Marx explained how any society was dominated by the class that controlled the dominant means of production. Under capitalism, profits were extracted by the difference in price between the costs of raw materials and labor, and the price goods sold for. Workers needed to be paid only enough to "reproduce" their labor for the next day's work, just enough for food, shelter, and clothing, as well as the bare maintenance of a household that would produce the next generation of workers. (Women's domestic work was assumed to be free.) Besides being squeezed by extraction of the surplus value of their labor, members of the working class were alienated from the products of their labor. In assembly-line work, where each repetitively made only parts of objects, final products did not reflect workers or what they could have expressed through more natural forms of work. (Marx's idea of this potentially redeeming role of natural work built on Hegel's idea of the importance of recognition through work.) It is ironic that the major communist revolutions in the 20th century occurred in predominantly agricultural nations such as Russia, China, and Cuba.

Marx's theory of history as determined by control of the means of production did not have room for a positive conception of democratic government, because it entailed that violent revolution was necessary to reach a stateless goal that would benefit erstwhile workers. Nevertheless, Marx's focus on those who labored, who were the majority of Europeans and Americans, was democratic, because it was about the interests and power of those who were or would be the *demos* under democratic government—the people.

Although Marx himself thought in terms of revolution and inspired violent overthrow of existing governments, some of his radical thought became part of the political culture of stable liberal democracies. This Marxist legacy of Social Democracy became the modus operandi of labor unions and led to progressive goals of expanded "safety net" programs under capitalist economic systems. When Marx wrote, neither women nor the laboring class could vote in the United States and Europe, but Social Democracy became increasingly feasible as suffrage expanded. With or without ideas of foundational rights or progress through democratic institutional processes, the end goal, that everyone should have enough money to live and flourish within a capitalistic system, became an enduring component of further conceptions of democracy.

American 19th-century reform movements

Within contemporary conceptions of democracy, there is no place for slavery, suffrage restriction of women and minorities, child labor, racial and gender discrimination, and voter suppression. Globally, the persistence of these ills means that universal human rights, whether religious, humanitarian, or guaranteed by government, have not been secured. These rights, and others, were fully promulgated for the first time in 1948 in the United Nations Universal Declaration of Human Rights (UDHR). Many now take them for granted as democratic norms. But the United States required at least a century of struggle to begin to implement them. Some of that implementation was inspired by Bentham, Mill, and Marx, but the societal and legal changes required for actualization were also the results of social and political organization and movements that often emerged from grass-roots aspirations.

In the United States and throughout the Anglo-influenced world, the practical efforts toward abolitionism and women's suffrage were intertwined with the Temperance Movement. This resulted in US Prohibition from 1920 to 1933 and Canadian from 1918 to 1920, as well as prohibition throughout India from 1947, which is still in place in some states there. Religion was also an important factor in 19th- and 20th-century reform movements in the United States that addressed education and public health. As a result of the Second Great Awakening of the 1820s and 1830s, by 1845, the number of Christian ministers in the United States increased to 40,000 from 2,000 in 1770. New religious and secular institutions arose during the period. Joseph Smith founded the Mormon Church (The Church of Jesus Christ of Latter-Day Saints), based on gold plates he claimed to have unearthed in western New York. Projects to create utopian communities as a reaction against industrialization and commercialism included Brook Farms, founded by New England Transcendentalists, and the Oneida Colony, which stressed individual sexual freedom (and became the Oneida Silver Company).

Historians disagree about whether the main cause of the American Civil War was the societal battle over slavery, or if it was state secession versus national unity. In either case, states that attempted to secede were pro-slavery and the Union cause became explicitly abolitionist after the Emancipation Proclamation of 1863. The Civil War was historically greater than any reform movement because it resulted in definitive changes in the US Constitution: slavery was abolished, and former male slaves eventually became citizens.

The Civil War had been preceded by the abolitionist and women's suffrage movements, both of which were socially, as well as politically, progressive. Before the US Civil War, in the United States and Britain, leaders in the abolitionist movement against black chattel slavery joined forces with the women's rights movement and vice versa. This alliance was fractured in the United States when black men got the right to vote under the 15th Amendment in 1870. Racial discrimination in the United States then splintered the women's suffrage movement, both among white suffragists and between white and black suffragists generally. Nineteenth-century white women's rights leaders such as Susan B. Anthony and Elizabeth Cady Stanton resented African American men getting the right to vote before they did, although others in the movement supported the Emancipation Amendments. Anthony and Stanton founded the National Woman Suffrage Association (NWSA) in 1869, but women were not granted suffrage in the US until 1920 (two years after Britain) (Figure 6). African American women were excluded from white women's political groups and social clubs after the Civil War. They then formed their own, but well into the 20th century, the

CHARACTER SKETCHES AT THE WOMEN'S SUFFRAGE MEETING AT ST. JAMES'S HALL

6. **Vintage engraving of sketches from the Women's Suffrage meeting at St James's Hall, London, 1884.**

suppression of black votes under Jim Crow laws blocked their suffrage in the US South.

The United States never developed a political Labor Party, as did countries throughout Europe and other parts of the world. Membership in US labor unions declined from 20 percent of workers in 1983. By 2021, just 12.1 percent of American workers were represented by unions, compared to 82 percent in Sweden and 35 percent in Italy (although only 9 percent in Turkey). Some critics have claimed that the US working class has continually been divided by race, to the benefit of capitalist exploiters who take advantage of racism to symbolically pay poor white workers part of their wages through recognition of their white racial status (called "the wages of whiteness"). Wages for blacks and other people of color have been even less.

Inadequate and segregated education, as well as outright exclusion from higher education until the mid-20th century, has been a trans-generational barrier for entry into the middle and leadership classes for African Americans and other non-white groups. The gains for labor were largely limited to workers in skilled trades. From colonial times until the Massachusetts Supreme Judicial Court 1842 decision in *Commonwealth v Hunt*, worker "combinations" (which evolved into unions) were illegal. By the end of the century, railroad unions and the American Federation of Labor (AFL) were formed, and by 1905, the United Mine Workers, The Women's Trade Union League, and the Industrial Workers of the World.

Left out of 19th-century reform in the United States was just treatment of indigenous peoples, who had been removed from their ancestral lands and faced annihilation of their cultures. Some of their political and social practices could have been important contributions to American (and international) conceptions of democracy. This disregard had been set in the 18th century. The Iroquois Confederacy had a federal system of government that inspired a disparaging mention by Benjamin Franklin in a 1751 letter:

> It would be a very strange thing if Six Nations of Ignorant Savages should be capable of forming a Scheme for such a Union and be able to execute it in such a manner, as that it has subsisted Ages, and appears indissoluble and yet a like Union should be impracticable for ten or a dozen English colonies, to whom it is more necessary, and must be more advantageous.

The political position of women in Iroquois government could also have been a foundation for the US women's movement. Instead, suffragists relied on more abstract writings by Mary Wollstonecraft and John Stuart Mill to overcome the British common law doctrine of *coverture* from Blackstone's Commentaries. (According to Blackstone, married women had no financial or other independent rights but were "covered" by their husbands as the sole rights' bearers.) The Iroquois constitution or Great Law of Peace specified that Iroquois clans were matriarchal by descent. Men moved into the houses of their mothers-in-law after marriage. Clan Mothers, chosen by other adult women, had the highest decision-making authority. They could depose male *Sachems* or chiefs, who were accountable to them. Both Benjamin Franklin and other founding fathers were aware of these practices but did not consider the possibility of women's political citizenship when they wrote the US Constitution.

Social progressivism and history

Neither utilitarian moral theory nor Marxism explicitly issued from political conceptions of democracy or ideas about the structures of democratic government. Bentham saw no validity in the idea of rights; Mill was skeptical of majority rule; and Marx thought that democracy was dominated by an oppressive class. The social reform movements in 19th-century America were more influenced by religion than utilitarianism or Marxism. Nevertheless, the spirit of these movements came from the *demos*, those who were ruled under existing democratic government structures. The movements emerged against conditions that many recognized as intolerable, such as slavery. Movement leaders resisted settled custom under common law and governmental structures. The labor movement also had to struggle against settled law that prohibited unions, as well as employer interests that opposed them.

In sum, the ideas motivating reform processes did not arise from prevailing conceptions of democracy. However—and this introduced a new conduit for change within democracy—utilitarianism, Marxism, and Christianity applied moral insights to demands for political change. Such *political morality* did not always result in legal changes, although sometimes it did, as in the abolition of slavery and women's suffrage. Political morality also contributes to new conceptions of democracy, by extending democracy from government structure to societal reorganization toward equality. Groups previously excluded benefit thereby, and the moral political universe is expanded for members of dominant groups, because they are now required to recognize and respect members of subordinate groups. Overarching beliefs in progress ground the idea that such reform is possible.

Twentieth-century social progressivism was also to rely on optimism that life could be better for some groups in society. In established democracies, rising groups have been successful due to democratic constitutional rights to freedom of speech and assembly. Moreover, the utilitarian insight that pleasure and happiness are good, and pain and suffering bad, continues to inform contemporary conceptions of democracy. Marxism is also an ongoing influence in contemporary furtherance of the well-being of workers, as is the persisting Jeffersonian idea that extreme income inequality is detrimental to democracy.

Chapter 7
New democracies and new conceptions of democracy

Few veterans of World War II and Holocaust survivors remain. Soon, there will be no one left to provide first-hand accounts. World War II put worldwide democracy on the line during the enormously destructive events from September 1, 1939 to September 2, 1945. Between 35 and 60 million people were killed. Six million Jews and as many Catholics, Romas, people with disabilities, and non-German nationals were murdered ("exterminated") in concentration camps. German forces invaded and occupied most of continental Europe and Japan made conquests in Indochina and the Pacific (Figure 7).

Some countries changed sides during the war. Germany led the Axis Powers of Italy, Japan, Hungary, Romania, and Bulgaria. The Allies, led by Britain and the United States, were joined by France, the USSR, Australia, Belgium, Brazil, Canada, China, Denmark, Greece, the Netherlands, New Zealand, Norway, Poland, South Africa, and Yugoslavia. As the war progressed, Italy, Japan, and Germany were invaded by the Allies, mainly the United States, Great Britain, France, the USSR, and China. European cities, as well as railways and bridges, were devastated. Imperial powers brought their colonies into the war with them and India alone provided 2.5 million troops; West Africa, Gambia, Sierra Leone, the Gold Coast (now Ghana), and Nigeria held allied military bases or staging areas, as did countries in the Middle East.

7. Flying military airplanes and machine guns.

Sixty million civilians were displaced. The monetary cost was estimated to exceed that of all wars since medieval times. (The expense to the United States was about 4 trillion in current dollars.) The devastation of Europe left two superpowers, the USSR and the US, which were soon to engage in a long cold war.

Toward preventing another world war, immediately after World War II, the Allies imposed new democratic political structures on the governments of Germany, Italy, and Japan. As well, some countries were able to autonomously revise their governments toward democracy, and newly constituted independent former colonies had opportunities to form their own governments, although their conceptions of democracy were often inherited from former colonizers. The majority adopted parliamentary systems with proportional representation, but most emulated the US Constitution in their founding documents. Twenty-four new, autonomous republics were formed from 1944 to 1950: Iceland, North Korea, South Korea, Indonesia, Vietnam, Taiwan, Bosnia and Herzegovina, Croatia, Macedonia, Montenegro, Serbia, Slovenia, Albania, Hungary, Italy, Bulgaria, the Marshall Islands, the Federated States of Micronesia, Palau, Romania, Myanmar, Israel, Ireland, and India. The decades after World War II also saw internal changes toward greater democracy in India, the United States, and South Africa.

The war had followed the rise of *fascism*, which was in many ways the antithesis of democracy, and political theorists of the period were very aware of fascism as a future threat. But before the term "fascism" itself became opprobrious, theorists of fascism such as the Hegelian Italian philosopher Giovanni Gentile (1875–1944) claimed that only fascist governments could truly represent the people, because they were honest about inequalities and their leaders could express the universal will of the electorate. German philosopher Martin Heidegger, playwright Luigi Pirandello, American theorists Eric Voegelin and Leo Strauss (who were refugees from Germany and Austria), and German legal scholar Carl Schmitt had also turned to fascism in their criticism of contemporary democracy. They all expressed support for the fascist leadership of Germany and Italy before Adolf Hitler and Benito Mussolini came to full power. However, they backed away as the war advanced. Progressive conceptions of democracy following World War II were opposed to the fascist ideology of racial superiority and strong militaristic government, which had preceded the war. Political theorists generally came to believe that fascist ideology was a major cause of the historical rise of Hitler and Mussolini.

Imposed changes into democracies

Democratic governments proclaim and practice free elections, individual rights to free speech, assembly, and religion, and limits and checks to government power. Democracy is dynamic, because it allows for construction, reconstruction, and degeneration. Conceptions of democracy, which are often aspirational, can come before or after the events they describe. But there are no magic words here. New conceptions of democracy require acceptance, implementation in law, and application in policy.

After World War II, the Axis countries at first had democratic reforms externally imposed. The US-financed Marshall Plan enabled both West Germany and Japan to embark on economic recovery, under restrictions to their rearmament and requirements that their government structures become more democratic. Nazi war criminals were prosecuted, tried, and punished in the Nuremberg Trials (and 12 were sentenced to death). In 1949, the Basic Law became the founding document for the Federal Republic of Germany that was then West Germany, the territory under control of Western Allies United States, United Kingdom, and France; the Soviet Union had control over East Germany. In 1957, the German Republic along with France, Italy, and the Benelux countries formed the European Economic Community. The German Republic held free elections and party politics flourished, resulting in democratic government stable enough to support the reunification of Soviet-controlled East Germany with West Germany, into the nation of Germany, in 1990.

During World War II, Italy had left the Axis powers and joined the Allies in 1944. The Italian Resistance movement included opposition to Mussolini's fascism, national liberation against the Nazi occupation, and struggles of socialists and communists against capitalists. Following the war, women were enfranchised and in 1946, a popular vote chose a parliamentary republic, without a monarchy.

Although Japan's democracy was also externally required, it did not have the full benefits of the international alliances that the European Axis nations could join. The Japanese military had taken over the country during the 1930s. Japan's 1937 invasion of China led to deterioration of its relations with the United States, which culminated in Japan's 1941 attack on Pearl Harbor. Four years after the United States entered World War II, in 1945, it dropped atomic bombs on Hiroshima and Nagasaki. (Japan remains the only nation to have endured nuclear attack.)

The goals of the US Japanese occupation after the war were democratization and demilitarization. A new constitution was promulgated in 1947, with a democratically elected House of Councilors and relegation of the emperor's status to symbolic representation of the Japanese people. A number of democratic reforms were imposed: women were given equal rights to men; freedom of religion, press, assembly, and speech were established; the formation of labor unions was encouraged; large landholdings were redistributed to abolish tenant farming. A multi-party system with proportional representation evolved, but so did a national bureaucracy with positions based on merit, albeit dominated by graduates of elite universities. This bureaucracy developed the function of designing policies, but elected representatives accepted, rejected, or negotiated them. (This structure fulfilled John Stuart Mill's vision from about a century earlier—see Chapter 6.)

Arendt, Popper, Rawls, and Sen

New 20th-century democratic political thought was informed by threats to democracy raised by World War II and communist totalitarianism after the war. While the contributions of key thinkers did not directly cause democratic progress, they provided a background against which subsequent more activist projects could be effective. Hannah Arendt's writings on democracy ran counter to modern emphases on representation and majority rule and seemed to call for a revival of the tradition of classical republicanism. Karl Popper emphasized the importance of empirical principles for governing. John Rawls stressed the importance of an ideal of justice as fairness in major societal institutions. The abstract nature of Rawls's theory was countered by Amartya Sen's *capabilities approach* to economic distribution. Arendt and Popper were reacting to World War II, but Rawls and Sen, writing several decades later, were addressing present and future supports for democracy. Except for Sen (whose ideas have been practically applied in third world development projects), these thinkers did not have direct, evident influence on democratic changes. But their insights continue to motivate political and social discussion, sometimes among those who do have the power to initiate change.

German-American political and social philosopher Hannah Arendt (1906–75) had to leave Germany and then France during World War II, because of her Jewish ancestry. Her experience of totalitarianism motivated key ideas in at least two of her works, *The Human Condition* (1958) and *On Revolution* (1963). Arendt proposed public councils in a revision of democratic society that was neither individually liberal nor socially collectivist. Democratic councils would be participatory forums for citizens to discuss and form their political views, as an essential part of their civic life. This public sphere would be an actual space allowing for citizens' collective political identity to form through dialogue, although its actual location need not be specified in advance of people coming together. Opinions, as distinct from factual truth, needed to be expressed. Arendt saw no place for racial and ethnic identities in the public political forum. This exclusion likely stemmed from her negative experience of Nazi propaganda about Aryan superiority. More generally, Arendt believed that the modern, materialistic expansion into shared public life of activities and goods that were formerly relegated to private life had eclipsed authentic political participation. Drawing from Kant, she wrote that "we think, as it were, in community with others to whom we communicate our thoughts as they communicate theirs to us."

Austrian-born philosopher of science Karl Popper (1902–94) also had his life disrupted by the Nazis. He relocated to New Zealand before writing his opposition to political tyranny in *The Open Society and its Enemies* (1945), and later settled in England. With *Conjectures and Refutations: The Growth of Scientific Knowledge* (1972), Popper became famous for his distinction of scientific claims as being capable of *falsification*: Beliefs or hypotheses that could not be falsified could not be scientific. Beliefs and hypotheses that withstood attempts to falsify them were "corroborated," rather than proved true. Popper criticized Marxists and Freudians as unscientific, because they did not permit their predictions to be falsified by empirical evidence. He argued that the "open society" was required to protect individual freedom, especially free oppositional speech. His conception of democratic government was that it should consist of piecemeal, problem-solving policies that could be abandoned if results falsified predictions.

In *A Theory of Justice* (1970), American political philosopher John Rawls (1921–2002) provided a new liberal—I would say "progressive"—social-contract foundation for societies that were already "well-ordered" in having democratic traditions and citizens who were law-abiding. Although his work was part of the social contract tradition, his "original position" was not the state of nature posited by Hobbes, Locke, and Rousseau. Rather, deliberation about the basic institutions of government and society were to be imagined in a thought experiment. Rawls thereby embarked on *ideal theory*, reasoning that it was necessary to have a model of justice in order to correct injustice—"The principles of justice (in lexical order) belong to ideal theory."

Rawls began with the claim that justice was the first political virtue, and the concept of justice was universally approved. However, this general concept required specific conceptions and Rawls's conception was *justice as fairness*. In his thought experiment, stakeholders from a society would design major institutions behind a "veil of ignorance," so that they were not to know their own wealth, status, identities, life plans, psychology, and talents. On the principle that one child cuts the cake and another chooses their piece, this ignorance was to preclude stakeholders from furthering their own interests in their designs of societal institutions. There were also provisos: public offices would be open to all; and the *difference principle* required that although inequalities were acceptable, there could not be changes that worsened the circumstances of those already worse off. Each was to have as much liberty as was compatible with the liberty of others.

Critics objected that Rawls's ideal theory did not apply to the United States because of its persistent inequalities, especially concerning race. Some of Rawls's American followers therefore sought to approach the conditions for justice through *nonideal theory*, or the application of a Rawlsian thought experiment to a society that is not well ordered. But not all were satisfied with that strategy. Indian Nobel Laureate economist and political philosopher Amartya Sen (b. 1933), who was a student and then a colleague of Rawls at Harvard University, developed the *capabilities approach* for welfare economics instead of ideal theory. In his 2009 *The Idea of Justice*, Sen advocated a focus on "actualization" in people's real lives. He dismissed the importance of a focus on structures, in what he called Rawlsian "transcendental institutionalism." As an example, Sen pointed out that in choosing between a painting by Dalí and one by Picasso, it is irrelevant whether the *Mona Lisa* is the most perfect picture in the world. This meant that Rawlsian ideal justice is irrelevant if we have to choose between nonideal alternatives. Also, drawing on Sanskrit literature, Sen distinguished between *niti* or "organizational propriety and behavioural correctness" and *nyaya* or "the world that actually emerges." Similar to Popper who thought that the goal of social-political life should be to minimize suffering, rather than increase happiness, Sen proposed minimizing injustice.

Sen's capabilities approach focused on what disadvantaged people were capable of utilizing, in place of uniform distributions of goods or services that might not be useful and beneficial to them. For instance, Sen witnessed starvation during the Bengal famine of 1943 and in his 1981 *Poverty and Famines: An Essay on Entitlement and Deprivation*, he explained that this was not the result of either a lack of food or interference with the right to buy food, but a lack of capability to buy food. Sen's idea of *capabilities* introduced positive rights in contrast to negative rights that were merely freedom from interference. Capabilities are what people are actually free to do. In the Bengal famine, many were not free to buy food, simply because they did not have enough money.

Internal democratic developments

Internal developments of democracy have often resulted from popular movements with charismatic leaders. In the 20th century, remarkable democratic progress was inspired by Mohandas Gandhi in India, Martin Luther King in the United States, and Nelson Mandela in South Africa. For India, democratic government combined both independence from Great Britain and a continuation of existing democratic structures and practices. In both the United States and South Africa, inclusive democracy has been an application to non-whites of rights and recognition already accorded to whites. Gandhi inspired King and both inspired Mandela.

India is now the most populous global democracy, with almost 1.4 billion in 2021. India became an independent state in 1947 and its democratic institutions have endured. Mohandas Karamchand Gandhi (1869–1948) led the successful movement for independence with astute moral pragmatism.

Gandhi studied law in England and then went to South Africa, where he became an activist advocate for the rights of Indians in that British colony. Using civil disobedience with nonviolent protest, he was able to mobilize thousands toward reform of racially discriminatory laws against Indians. He returned to India in 1915. The Indian National Congress, widely known as the Congress Party, already had the goal of independence from Great Britain. Gandhi's genius lay in recognizing the power of peaceful, righteous, mass protest and he applied what he had learned in

South Africa to India. He deflected the Congress Party from lawyers' legal reform projects aiming for changes in legislation and court decisions, to activism that included the masses in civil disobedience. Millions protested, went on strike, and were jailed. Gandhi rejected violence on Hindu religious grounds that it was wrong to harm living creatures. British military forces could have prevailed over violent insurrection, but they were withdrawn in the face of peaceful opposition that was morally motivated. Ethnic and religious conflict between majority Hindus and minority Muslims could not be reconciled, however. At the time of India's independence, Pakistan was partitioned off as a separate nation, with two-thirds of 100 million Muslims leaving India. Gandhi was assassinated by a Hindu nationalist in 1948.

Although the immense popular and reverential status of Gandhi became symbolic of Indian democracy, India's pre-existing federalism and democratic institutions were the basis of democratic political stability. The British East India Company had entered with commercial interests in the 1600s, and by 1857 it defeated the French for political control. At that time, the British monarchy took power over the country and while modern infrastructure (roads, railways, telegraphs, and irrigation) was instituted, the world contribution of the Indian economy drastically declined. Direct rule was supposed to allow for consultation with Indians, but the period of Britain's rule mainly supported its dependence on Indian raw materials, especially cotton. The Indian National Congress arose in 1885, with the aim of democratic national autonomy.

After India's independence, Cambridge-educated, modern-thinking Jawaharlal Nehru (1889–1964) became prime minster and government policy was democratically decided by the judiciary in cases of conflict. Power was peacefully transferred after parliamentary and state elections. The press was free to voice opposition. While ethnic conflicts between Hindus and Muslims, and Hindus and Sikhs frequently erupted, the Congress Party was committed to ethnic inclusion and compromise. In addition, ethnic conflicts did not spread throughout India, but remained limited to the states in which they erupted. The army remained professional and restrained, without intervening in local political disputes.

Race relations in the United States perpetuated inequality and social disadvantage for African Americans, well into the 20th century. In 1954, Martin Luther King Jr. (1929–68) became minister of the Dexter Avenue Baptist Church in Montgomery, Alabama. He emulated Gandhi's method of passive resistance through public protest, and also rejected violence on religious and strategic grounds. Politically, King's core idea was to apply the rights already enjoyed by white Americans to black Americans. King garnered global attention in organizing a boycott of Montgomery buses, after Rosa Parks refused to comply with segregationist law and sit in the back of a bus. King founded the Southern Christian Leadership Conference and organized the March on Washington, DC, in 1963. This was the occasion of his "I Have a Dream" speech, when he urged white Americans to fulfil their egalitarian founding promises so that his children would "not be judged by the color of their skin, but by the content of their character." King stood behind President Johnson when he signed the Voting Rights Act in 1965. He then announced a Poor People's Campaign in 1968, but he was assassinated that same year by a white segregationist (although some members of his family believed that the FBI had set him up).

Race relations in the United States have been an ongoing site of conflict and controversy. While segregation is no longer lawful in public places, by the early 21st century, residential segregation has not fallen from its 1970s peak, especially pertaining to African Americans. Causes include white preferences for de facto segregation and the lack of political will to enforce the 1968 Fair Housing Act that outlawed racial discrimination in housing sales, rentals, and financing. Gaps between blacks and whites are entrenched throughout American society, in wealth, income, education, and health. Unjustified police killings of unarmed black people continue to capture national news. During the COVID-19 pandemic, African Americans have disproportionately died, and their numbers in the criminal justice system remain disproportionately high.

Hispanic/Latinx and Native Americans also continue to suffer disproportionately from inequalities accompanying their non-white racial status. Asian Americans have been scapegoated in acts of violence motivated by the association of China with the origin of the SARS-CoV-2 virus. While progressive voices and public protest continue to be heard and seen, this overall undemocratic racial inequality has so far proven intransigent. There have been incremental gains that include rising middle classes in every non-white racial and ethnic group, but they are insufficient to solve or resolve the underlying persistence of racial prejudice and discrimination among substantial numbers of white Americans.

South Africa and Nelson Mandela

Democracy in South Africa was similar to the United States in its history of exclusive representational democratic structures for white males, although there it was British and Dutch colonizers. The Cape of Good Hope was first colonized by Dutch traders and settlers in the mid-1600s. In the early 1800s, a British colony was founded, and settlers arrived. Both Afrikaners and British practiced white racial dominance against the Khoisan, Xhosa, and Zulu peoples, and imported Malay slaves. The British abolished the slave trade in the early 1800s and emancipated all slaves in 1834.

Afrikaner nationalists retrenched following British victory in the Boer War of 1902. The Afrikaner Nationalist Party was victorious in 1948 and they established a republic in 1960. From the early

1900s, black tribal groups had pushed for political representation through the African National Congress (ANC). Over decades, the ANC made moderate demands for political representation. They were ignored by the British and crushed by Afrikaner white supremacist rule. Afrikaners strictly excluded blacks from their churches and governments, whereas educated, property-owning blacks had been enfranchised by the British. By the 1940s, the ANC openly resisted *apartheid*, which restricted members of tribal groups who were the overwhelming majority of the population to substandard segregated "homelands." After 1948, the ANC was permitted to function, but its demands continued to be ignored.

In 1960, 200 black Africans were wounded or killed at the Sharpeville Massacre, and the Republic of South Africa banned the ANC and enacted oppressive security laws. By 1971, each black South African was assigned to one of 10 homelands that made up 13 percent of the national territory. Black homelands lacked infrastructure for adequate education and employment, and civic participation rights were restricted to whites within the rest of the country. Concessions were made to "colored" (mixed-race) and Asian populations, but this led to more protests. The white government declared a state of emergency from 1986 to 1990.

International indignation over apartheid was intense. External economic sanctions depleted South Africa and negotiations between the government and the ANC began in 1990. It took three years for the government of President F. W. de Klerk (1936–2021) to agree that apartheid was morally unacceptable. Militants within the ANC were by then reluctant to compromise, but there was finally a universal election on May 9, 1994. The ANC gained 62 percent of the vote, which enabled it to govern, although it did not have power to control the new constitution. Nelson Mandela (1918–2013) was then president of the ANC and he became the first president of post-apartheid South Africa. Mandela devoted his entire life to activist and political work towards racial democracy and had not been deterred by numerous prison sentences.

In 1995, Mandela coordinated negotiations to include more extreme and militant members of the ANC and the (Afrikaner) Nationalist Party in the Truth and Reconciliation Commission (TRC). Chaired by Archbishop Desmond Tutu (1931–2021), the purpose of the TRC was to reveal the truth about human rights violations during apartheid, provide reparations to victims of violence, and create opportunities for both victims and perpetrators to relate their experiences during apartheid. However, unlike the Nuremberg Commission, the TRC did not have prosecutorial power. The TRC also contained an Amnesty Committee. There were over 22,000 statements and 7,000 amnesty hearings, with 1,500 granted amnesty for apartheid crimes. Reactions to the TRC have been mixed, with some lauding the genuine nature of the reconciliation it enabled and others decrying its lack of just punishment.

Reflections on political history and theory

Some thinkers, such as Plato, Machiavelli, Locke, Mill, and Sen, were directly influential in governmental affairs of their day. Others, such as Arendt, Popper, and Rawls, reacted to recent history, but their ineffable influence can be read into subsequent democratic progress in real history. Although political theory is not always simply or directly connected to real world history, there are not only commonalities between thought and events over the same time period, but some ideas themselves become part of history. The turbulence of World War II evoked new ideas that extended thought about democratic structure from government to society. As described in this chapter, some of the results were new conceptions of democracy for the contexts in which they were applied, including Indian independence as a democratic nation, civil rights legislation for African Americans, and the end of apartheid in South Africa. Moral political ideas for egalitarian society that had been developed in 19th-century thought were thus implemented.

To sum up. Arendt's idea of direct participatory democracy can be read in the great 20th-century liberation movements, although not in changed structures of democratic government, as she may have preferred. Although protesters and demonstrators do not have direct political power, they undoubtedly influence those who do. Rawls's work continues to remind many that all social identities should have a say in the form and functioning of basic institutions in society. And although Rawls is considered a political philosopher, his focus on institutions has been relevant to justice in society. Sen raised nuanced questions about just economic distribution in a world starkly divided between haves and have-nots. Popper's idea of evidence-based democratic government still lacks broad political popularity, although an exception may be times of emergency, such as the public health crises attending the COVID-19 pandemic, which many leaders have addressed by relying on scientific information. The pandemic affected minorities and the poor disproportionately, and drew attention to social inequalities that had been difficult to change in normal times. Such natural emergencies, like man-made war, may provide opportunities for expanding democracy, although at the same time, these upheavals can increase vulnerability to undemocratic regressions.

Chapter 8
The future of democracy: threats and resilience

Mature progressives often look to youth for inspiration. But when teenage Swedish climate activist Greta Thunberg addressed the United Nations in 2019, she was having none of it (Figure 8). Not wishing to inspire those same world leaders who were robbing youth of their future, she exclaimed, "How dare you!" Climate change is an indirect external global threat to democracy. As ever more extreme weather events destroy homes and infrastructure, and sea-level rise, loss of agricultural land, and intolerable temperatures cause millions to become refugees, political conflict and undemocratic measures, from emergency declarations to right-wing populism, will likely intensify.

Direct recent threats to democracy have been both internal and external to nations. The attack on the US Capitol on January 6, 2021 represented an internal threat, whereas the devastation of Ukrainian cities by Russian military forces has been an external threat. Conceptions of democracy developed by political theorists and activists are well established in an intellectual historical arc bending towards an expanding *demos* with greater social equality. That is, political theory can be interpreted as more democratic over time. But that is a matter of discourse. Some people will continue to say and write the right things, but the future of actual democracies is less predictable.

8. Greta Thunberg speaks at the United Nations, September 23, 2019.

In highly charged political conflict within democratic societies, both progressives and conservatives can claim that their opponents are threatening core institutions. In winner-takes-all election practices, as in the United States, there can be a see-saw effect of top-down changes, depending on which party is in power. It is therefore necessary to rely on standards for democratic rule that are politically neutral. These include free elections, an independent judiciary, freedom of the press, religious freedom, respect for rule by law, and individuals' rights to their persons and property. Such standards and institutions are popular and well established. But they have to be continually refreshed and re-accepted to support ongoing progress. Progress itself needs to be protected under rule by law. The alternative to rule by law includes rule by personality, rule by wealth, and misrule due to corruption or cronyism.

In their 2018 *How Democracies Die*, Harvard political scientists Steven Levitsky and Daniel Ziblatt chronicled the destruction of democratic institutions outside of the United States, as a cautionary account for the United States. Levitsky and Ziblatt describe different actors and movements, at different times, with a focus on Venezuela, Turkey, Hungary, and Russia. They emphasize the importance of restraint and toleration of political opposition, to preserve the spirit of the law. In addition to cultivating political virtues, they call for awareness when democratically elected officials use democratic structures to achieve undemocratic goals. In other words, democracy itself can be used to undermine democracy.

Contemporary journalism bears out Levitsky's and Ziblatt's claims. In a 2020 "Briefing" from *The Economist*, observers of the government of Prime Minister Narendra Modi in India recounted an erosion of checks and balances that appears to be a trend toward authoritarian rule. They noted slow judicial response to rights violations that overrode constitutional safeguards, including: the association of Indian national identity with Hindu religious identity; the institution of direct national rule over the state of Jammu and Kashmir; a growing tendency of the military to comment publicly on civilian issues; new arbitrary powers to label groups and individuals "terrorists"; police brutality against Muslim protesters; and unlimited anonymous donations to political parties. India so far continues to have free and orderly elections. However, Modi won re-election by a landslide in 2019 and his party was not censured for infractions of conduct codes, while opposing candidates were.

The threats to democracy in India arise from internal politics. External threats to democracy may be easier to recognize than internal ones. Everyone can see outright government takeover by another sovereign power, such as German invasions and occupation of other European countries during World War II, or a revolution or military coup with undemocratic goals. But there was democratic resistance to the Nazis throughout the war and the 2021 military coup in Myanmar was met by widespread public protest and work strikes. These kinds of resistance can be expected to continually arise, as possible and necessary. Their success depends on physical and moral force, and also external support. The world public has witnessed, almost in real time, how external support has been necessary for Ukraine's resistance to Russian invasion, which is ongoing as of this writing.

Natural disasters are another form of external threat, be they either weather related or biological or something as yet unknown. But the nature of destruction from such non-human events and conditions depends on how society is already constructed. Jean-Jacques Rousseau identified the socially constructed nature of the Lisbon earthquake of 1755, by noting that it would have been of little concern had it occurred in nature and that many would not have died had they not chosen to live in seven-story buildings or rush back into them to save their possessions. The 2020 COVID-19 pandemic made many throughout the world aware of a number of ordinary vulnerabilities that they had taken for granted: occupational and income inequalities; women's general job insecurity and childcare obligations; pre-existing disadvantages associated with race and ethnicity. Thus, socially structured inequalities, which are already undemocratic, become worse during disasters. Such threats to democracy from non-human causes thereby amount to threats from preexisting human causes. Insofar as climate change is caused by human fossil fuel consumption, the social construction of this disaster is self-evident. (Rousseau would have a field day: "They chose to produce and consume fast food at the cost of rain forests and their passionate love affairs with automobiles will be their ruin.")

How to think about democracy

The future of democracies as political conditions that actions in the present can shape depends on how internal and external threats are understood and met, as well as on aspirations and expectations that are already formed. The academic term *methodology* pertains to how specialized scholars approach the idea of democracy, but really it's a question of how we should all think about it and present that thought. In "Two Concepts of Liberty" (1958), Isaiah Berlin (1909–97) crystalized two democratic conceptions of liberty: negative liberty is protection from external interference; positive liberty is support for individuals' internal capabilities, or what they are able to do. Negative liberties are the familiar individual rights associated with classic democracies, whereas positive liberties are support for what individuals are able to do. Berlin cautioned against the "rhetorical abuse" of positive liberties and emphasized the role of different values in driving disputes about them. Progressive thought over the second half of the 20th century into the early 21st has supported positive liberties. For example, in the United States, there are presently no laws preventing poor and minority children from attending school and this is a negative liberty, as is their freedom to apply to colleges. But if their primary and secondary school education in poor neighborhoods has not taught them intellectual skills that are competitive among applicants from more advantaged environments, programs to help them scholastically would support their positive liberties (or capabilities in Amartya Sen's economic sense—see Chapter 7), so that their applications would be more likely to succeed.

The 1948 United Nations Universal Declaration of Human Rights (UDHR) was the first broadly accepted statement of universal human equality. It combined ideas of positive and negative liberties as described by Isaiah Berlin, but in the language of rights. UDHR specified freedom from rights violations (i.e., negative liberties) and freedom to enjoy the basics of a humane quality of life, through income, employment, rights to associate, rights to health and leisure, and special considerations for women and children (i.e., positive liberties). The UDHR has proved mainly aspirational, but its assertion of human equality was embedded in subsequent liberatory movements, such as the US civil rights movements and the end of apartheid.

Whether for protection of negative or positive rights or liberties, the passage of laws is not an ultimate process, because laws have to be applied or enforced in order to become real norms within both government and society. Conservatives may invoke accepted legal procedures in ways that can slow down or block the application of new egalitarian laws. The result is that equality in law does not immediately create equality in reality. Therefore, the whole of government, consisting of both laws and their application, may be viewed as one process.

American journalist and political theorist Arthur Bentley (1870–1957) emphasized this processual aspect of government in his 1908 *The Process of Government*. Bentley argued that social (or sociological) analyses of different groups and events in society required explanation in which "social events have social causes." That is, he insisted that study of societies needed to be conducted on the level of events happening within society, writing:

> If all this process of government were some "external" thing waiting to be pushed by feelings, or now and then pushing feelings in return, that would be one thing. But such is not the case. It is "internal," it is human, as much as anything we know of is internal and human.

Bentley added that external forces or biological differences cannot be used to account for the social disadvantages of some groups.

In discussing the situation of African Americans in the early 20th century, he wrote:

> I am not denying that men are in fact distinguished from one another by epithets relating to their intelligence and moral qualities; nor that different adults act differently in situations which we describe to ourselves as substantially the same; nor that this method of statement is useful in its own time and place. What I am asserting is that the attempt to erect it into a causal interpretation of society on the basis of fixed individual characters which can adequately be described and defined apart from the society they explain, is a hotbed of confusion and irrelevancy.

Bentley was not here commenting on the truth or falsity of the racist theories of race that abounded when he wrote but claiming that they were not conclusive or even relevant for studies of racial differences in society, which were social events and conditions requiring social causes. Twelve years before Bentley's *Process of Government* was published, African American philosopher and sociologist W. E. B. Du Bois (1868–1963) had made a similar methodological claim in his 1896 study *The Philadelphia Negro*. Du Bois showed empirically how the poverty, poor health, and high crime rates of his subjects were connected to housing restrictions, limited work opportunities, and substandard educational opportunities. In this way, Du Bois was able to concretely connect social causes with social effects.

Both Du Bois and Bentley were insisting that events and circumstances in society required further explanation also in terms of events and circumstances in society. Bentley generally rejected and blocked theoretical posits such as "biological racial inferiority," but Du Bois went a step further to identify discriminatory racist causes of gaps between white and black poverty, health, and crime. Bentley was interested in a view of government that included society, but Du Bois focused more directly on society itself.

Beyond distinctions such as Berlin's and methodological claims made by Du Bois and Bentley, history teaches us that a general statement of equality, even if official, is not sufficient to support the real equality of all members of the groups mentioned. After the general statement, specific inequalities affecting specific groups need to be explicitly brought to attention. This has been evident in US government through the need for the 1960s civil rights legislation, as well as proclamations of egalitarian ideals from the United Nations.

In terms of written law alone, the emancipation amendments to the US Constitution, adopted after the Civil War, should have given freed slaves and their descendants the same civil rights that whites had. But decades of social oppression and near-peonage in the US South, as well as the publicly approved practice of lynching, necessitated the civil rights legislation of the 1960s. Lynching was not outlawed on a federal level until it was designated a hate crime in March 2022.

The Civil Rights Act of 1964 made racial segregation illegal in public places and banned employment discrimination on the basis of race, color, religion, sex, or national origin. The Voting Rights Act of 1965 provided for federal observation of local election polls and penalties for voter registration obstruction. But even this legislation was no more the end of American racial inequality than the US Supreme Court ruling in *Brown v. Board of Education* that had outlawed segregation in education. Residential segregation continued, as did obstructions to voting rights. In a federal system in which public education is largely funded by property taxes, primary school education remains segregated by race, partly because minority students attend schools in poor neighborhoods that have inadequate resources. Laws alone have not ended racial inequality, because they are only the written part of the process of government. Public policy and social norms can easily dilute the practical effects of written laws, or else, large numbers of people may refuse to obey them.

The UN has since 1948 issued hundreds of declarations that affirm the rights of disadvantaged groups—women, racial and ethnic minorities, children, refugees, disabled people, LGBTQ+ people, and others—as though to specify and emphasize the applicability of universal rights in the UDHR. Also, despite its aspirational and inspirational role within rights-respecting democracies, the UN has continually found it necessary to negotiate with member nations whose governments violate the basic rights of citizens and residents. Neither specific declarations nor ongoing negotiations with members should have been necessary, because logically, UDHR is a universal reference to all human beings. However, the more specific reapplications of universal rights attest to the resilience of the universal project.

The concept of democracy, which is necessarily vague as a concept, means that those who are ruled have a say in rule, some voice in how they are ruled, what they can be told to do or not do, with punishment for noncompliance specified. Historically, democratic government has been appealing to members of nations or groups within nations who view themselves as both equal to and distinct from dominant groups but are not treated the same as dominant groups. The existing structures and processes of democratic government support optimism that the benefits of democracy can be extended to members of groups who are not treated equally with members of dominant groups. Progressive conceptions of democracy have the goal of expanding the numbers of those who are genuinely equal under democratic government. Progressives aspire and act to apply the principles of democracy to groups who are ruled but do not yet have a full say in that rule. Progressives thus seek to expand the real *demos*. Progressivism is both aspirational and applicative, and it remains incomplete.

Progressivism may be interrupted and regressed, depending on existing legal structures and laws, the character of officials, and the existing partial *demos*. Sometimes the interruption appears as a necessary curtailment of all rights in order to deal with an emergency. But at other times, regression is purely political, as a move to curtail the application of democratic principles to disadvantaged groups. However, history does not stop with either emergency or political regression, because there is always, even under the greatest repression of regression, progressive resistance. For example, anti-black and anti-Asian white supremacist violence in the United States during 2020 and 2021 has been consistently met with public demonstrations and protests, as well as local and federal government action to support the attacked groups. During the Ukraine invasion, a number of Russians have risked long prison terms to protest in public.

Epistemological threats

The term *epistemology* refers to what counts as knowledge and how people get knowledge. If government itself is a process, discussion on the basis of what is known is an important part of it. Parts of the *demos* newly included or working towards inclusion do not automatically know what they want government to do after they are full members of the participatory *demos*. They therefore need to talk among themselves and between themselves and more established members of the *demos*. Both 19th- and 20th-century thinkers theorized the importance of conversation and discussion, but in the early 21st century much of this "discourse" has been co-opted by pundits on sensational news media outlets, and posts and comments on social media. Apart from that, academic researchers sustain conversations and dialogues among themselves about what should be done and how decisions should be made. But that dimension of discourse is often en-bubbled. The persistence of democracy will likely depend on the nurturance and protection of more informed discussion within the broad electorate. This is the old issue of the requirement of education to sustain democracy, as well as understand what it is. Inclusive discussion among those with opposing views is particularly important, calling for flexible resilience.

Discussion enables those governed to have a say in governing, not on the basis of the same opinions and interests, but with a shared basis of truth about verified facts, so they can talk to one another with hope and expectation that opinions can change. There needs to be widespread common sense regarding the basis on which different interests can be pursued and opinions formed and argued. Ancient political theorists tended to dismiss democracy because they thought the *demos* was ignorant. Modern political theorists have stressed the importance of an educated electorate. Events and trends in the United States during the Trump administration, in the United Kingdom during Brexit, and in Germany after the admission of large numbers of Syrian refugees, have revealed epistemological weak points that can undermine public democratic discourse. Unsubstantiated rumors, conspiratorial narratives, and so-called "big lies" from leaders require fresh consideration. Large numbers of the *demos* are not only uninformed but do not agree with those who are informed about how to become informed. Those uninformed do not share the standards the informed hold for knowledge, particularly scientific conclusions. Science itself is now too easily dismissed, without serious understanding of its importance for knowledge.

Democracy became strained during the 2020 US presidential election. Conspiracy theories about politics and the COVID-19 pandemic abounded, not only within the United States but throughout the world. While belief in conspiracy theories has been associated with under-education, education is cognitive, and conspiracy theories without factual foundations may bypass cognition and activate emotional responses. There is political tension between those whose beliefs are based on evidence, with respect for expert opinion, and those who eschew evidence and contemn experts. The result is that existing tensions cannot be relaxed through orderly, rational discussion, because one side will not participate. Standing disputes thereby devolve into rhetorical battles that can ignite violence.

Those who study conspiracy theories emphasize how they are impermeable to both disconfirming facts and logical argument. This means that conspiracy thinking and the action it motivates cannot be addressed in the usual way, so that how they are addressed requires resilience. The usual way of democratic discussion with free speech protections generally applies John Stuart Mill's arguments against censorship in *On Liberty* (See chapter 6). Mill claimed that all points of view should be freely expressed, including morally wrong or factually incorrect ones, because arguing against them based on fact and logic ensures that one does not hold one's own valid opinions out of mere habit or superstition. Mill was concerned about individual epistemology or how people think that they come to know various things. His insight was that the conclusions of knowledge cannot be simply filed away—we need to continually go over our own reasoning. This last is a critical skill that can be taught in elementary and secondary school. But when adult citizens in democracies reject such rational processes and cling to beliefs that cannot be argued against, reasoning with logic about facts is ineffective for changing their minds.

Some conspiracy theories threaten the orderly political functioning of democracy: For instance, unscientific responses to the COVID-19 pandemic by the Trump administration in 2020, and widespread refusal to accept Trump's defeat in the 2020 election, in spite of overwhelming evidence. The results were incalculable disease spread and disruption of a usual and orderly transition to the new administration. There was a constant verbal battle between those who accepted mitigation methods of avoiding SARS-CoV-2 infection and others who insisted on their liberty to flout them. Later on, there was intense opposition between those who insisted on the accuracy of duly recorded electoral votes and those, including the then president's supporters in the US Senate and House of Representatives, who denied it. In such situations, those who depend on facts and logic to fuel political discourse are faced with a trilemma: Continue to argue rationally (but ineffectively); give up; or call for censorship of the uninformed opposition.

Karl Popper thought that it was generally acceptable to be intolerant toward those who refused to be tolerant, or undemocratic toward those who were undemocratic. But, like Mill, he thought intolerance and yearnings for authoritarianism could be addressed through rational discussion. Along with some conspiracy theorists, conservative populists who extoll nativism and white racial supremacy are intolerant. As arguments, their views can be addressed with the usual arsenal of fact and logic and a small percentage may be receptive to such efforts. But conspiracy-inspired beliefs usually do not yield to such rational address. How ought they to be addressed? The traditional dilemma for authorities in democracies is either to behave undemocratically by censoring the expression of such beliefs or allow them to play out. Free speech traditions favor the latter.

Intolerance of those who are intolerant is straightforward when violence has been committed, as crime or insurrection. But it is not helpful when it is believed that violence *may* ensue from irrational beliefs, although it has not yet occurred. Indeed, while this worry about the use of falsehood to incite violence was widely voiced toward the end of 2020 in the United States, there was neither censorship nor preemptive violence. After the assault on the US Capitol on January 6, 2021, criminal investigations and prosecutions followed. But a proactive protection of democracy requires active preventative measures, including new ones.

Popper also criticized the history of political philosophy for its perennial question of who should rule. Instead, Popper proposed that the question should be, "How do we get rid of bad government?" Popper's answer was that election day was "the great day of judgement." However, this is to assume that all of those eligible are free to vote and that all understand what they are voting for. This brings us to the importance of critical thinking in primary school curricula. But that takes a long time and often cannot overcome parental obstruction in local school systems. What may be needed is new adult education, although how to make that democratically both voluntary and popular is a challenging question. If new adult education is imposed or legally required, it will have the same structure as the undemocratic practices of indoctrination or forced propaganda.

The dilemma concerning public falsehoods is more nuanced and subtle than the line between speech and violence. There may be assumptions throughout a culture which encourage conspiracy thinking when unwanted events occur. Such assumptions can be challenged. For instance, backlash against African American progress can be interrogated and countered with claims that success is not a zero-sum game; and white anxiety about non-white electoral majorities can be allayed with reminders of the democratic rights of numerical minorities. Perhaps political and social leaders could be less optimistic and laudatory about their nation and policies. Needed might be expression of pessimism in future projections and deflationary humility about what leaders can do for the people. The result could be reduced expectations that reduce disappointment, shock, rage, and denial when a major natural disaster occurs, a depression unfolds, a pandemic arrives, or one's candidate loses an election. It is only an assumption that the world is a safe place, with ongoing well-being and prosperity for some special and perhaps dominant group, that creates a demand for extraordinary, conspiratorial explanations of unwanted, unforeseen events.

The preservation of democracy that is threatened by irrational conspiracy thinking might depend on honest, realistic, public messaging for adults. Given free speech rights and related liberties, such messaging will need to be described in attractive and engaging ways that leave its consumption optional. This importance of adult information would ideally be connected to how children are educated in preparation for civic life. The future of democracy within present democracies will likely hinge on whether the majority of the electorate is sufficiently informed to tell the difference between good and bad government, on the basis of their ability to accept unwanted reality.

Internationalism, indigenism, and a future conception of democracy

Because democracy has become an internationally recognized ideal of government and democratic societies have shown a trend toward social equality, it makes sense to consider the global plight of those who are very disadvantaged. In Hobbes's terms, they are often the victims of a failure of government to protect them, but there is little evidence that military protection by external nations can work. (The failure of long, nation-building wars in Afghanistan provides a relevant series of examples.) The subject here is closer to *humanitarianism* as a general concern for human life and well-being, than to democracy as structures of government, or societies under specific national governments. The disadvantaged across the world need both the safety of physical peace and measures to quell their fears. According to the United Nations 1994 Human Development Report, the idea of *human security*, which envisions physical safety, as well as freedom from want or extreme poverty, may be more useful for progress than ideas of national or military security.

As a humanitarian ideal, human security is independent of ideals of democracy that have been and continue to be tied to nationalities and nation states, although it seems to ensure, for those who have it, many of the benefits of democracy as an ideal tied to nationalities and nation states. There is today no world government to create a federation of nation-state democracies and it is unlikely that such a political organization will develop in the foreseeable future. But in seeking to expand the benefits of democracy beyond national borders, human security may be an idea that is part of future conceptions of international and global democracy.

The democratic rights of indigenous peoples throughout the world have been neglected, according to both the UDHR and their legally stated treaty rights with those national governments in which they are dependent sovereignties. The United Nations issued its Declaration on the Rights of Indigenous Peoples (UNDRIP) that was adopted by the General Assembly on September 13, 2007, with 144 votes in favor of its adoption by the General Assembly, 11 abstentions, and 4 against. Those who voted against the UNDRIP were Australia, Canada, New Zealand, and the United States, which all have long histories of oppression of their indigenous populations, without reparation. (Work on the UNDRIP had begun in 1982 but was delayed due to concerns from some nations with indigenous claims to resources and self-determination.) The UN recognized global discrimination against indigenous peoples and asserted their human and political rights. It also specified that their treaty rights within nations were international issues. Whether the rights of indigenous peoples are addressed within nations or externally, they will be an important factor in the future actualization of democratic principles.

If conceptions of democracy are limited to national governmental structures, history suggests that democracies can endure with considerable inequality in their societies. Democratic government requires function according to laws. Within democratic nations, progressive ideals of equality within society require that the *demos* constantly expand until members of all groups can participate in government and expect equal treatment within society. While international relations are not united by binding law, existing democratic governments ought to extend the basic principles of democracy to their international relations, especially in interactions with the global poor and particularly to their legal and social relations with members of indigenous dependent sovereignties within their borders. This would be a trans-national conception of democracy and it could be developed by members of democratic nations who at the same time strive to extend democracy in their own nations. There is no rule of logic or moral principle to preclude work on both domestic and trans-national conceptions of democracy, by either the same or different individuals and groups.

Democratic humanitarian policies are an important goal for political morality. If political morality can extend to those in dire circumstances who are far away, the world will not only become more democratic, but the same humanitarian spirit could quell internal political and cultural divisions. Intolerance and tolerant or intolerant reactions to it could soften. Peace is a great benefit of democracy in all of its conceptions and extensions, at home as well as abroad. The great mass of the *demos*, both officially and potentially under government, generally does thrive during peace, and craves peace during conflict, turmoil, and disruption.

Appendix: US Bill of Rights, 1789; The Declaration of the Rights of Man and of the Citizen, 1789; UN Universal Declaration of Human Rights

US Bill of Rights Ratified by the states on December 15, 1791

Preamble—Congress of the United States begun and held at the City of New-York, on Wednesday the fourth of March, one thousand seven hundred and eighty- nine.

THE Conventions of a number of the States, having at the time of their adopting the Constitution, expressed a desire, in order to prevent misconstruction or abuse of its powers, that further declaratory and restrictive clauses should be added: And as extending the ground of public confidence in the Government, will best ensure the beneficent ends of its institution.

RESOLVED by the Senate and House of Representatives of the United States of America, in Congress assembled, two thirds of both Houses concurring, that the following Articles be proposed to the Legislatures of the several States, as amendments to the Constitution of the United States, all, or any of which Articles, when ratified by three fourths of the said Legislatures, to be valid to all intents and purposes, as part of the said Constitution; viz.ARTICLES in addition to, and Amendment of the Constitution of the United States of America, proposed by Congress, and ratified by the

Legislatures of the several States, pursuant to the fifth
Article of the original Constitution. Amendment.

I. Congress shall make no law respecting an establishment of religion, or prohibiting the free exercise thereof; or abridging the freedom of speech, or of the press; or the right of the people peaceably to assemble, and to petition the Government for a redress of grievances.Amendment.

II. A well regulated Militia, being necessary to the security of a free State, the right of the people to keep and bear Arms, shall not be infringed. Amendment.

III. No Soldier shall, in time of peace be quartered in any house, without the consent of the Owner, nor in time of war, but in a manner to be prescribed by law. Amendment.

IV. The right of the people to be secure in their persons, houses, papers, and effects, against unreasonable searches and seizures, shall not be violated, and no Warrants shall issue, but upon probable cause, supported by Oath or affirmation, and particularly describing the place to be searched, and the persons or things to be seized.

V. No person shall be held to answer for a capital, or otherwise infamous crime, unless on a presentment or indictment of a Grand Jury, except in cases arising in the land or naval forces, or in the Militia, when in actual service in time of War or public danger; nor shall any person be subject for the same offence to be twice put in jeopardy of life or limb; nor shall be compelled in any criminal case to be a witness against himself, nor be deprived of life, liberty, or property, without due process of law; nor shall private property be taken for public use, without just compensation.

VI. In all criminal prosecutions, the accused shall enjoy the right to a speedy and public trial, by an impartial jury of the State and district wherein the crime shall have been committed, which district shall have been previously ascertained by law, and to be informed of the nature and cause of the accusation; to be confronted with the witnesses against him; to have compulsory process for obtaining witnesses in his favor, and to have the Assistance of Suits at common law, where the value in controversy shall exceed twenty dollars, the right of trial by jury shall be preserved, and no fact tried by a jury, shall be otherwise re-examined in any Court of the United States, than according to the rules of the common law.

VII. In Suits at common law, where the value in controversy shall exceed twenty dollars, the right of trial by jury shall be preserved, and no fact tried by a jury, shall be otherwise reexamined in any Court of the United States, than according to the rules of the common law.

VIII. The powers not delegated to the United States by the Constitution, nor prohibited by it to the States, are reserved to the States respectively, or to the people.

The Bill of Rights Center for Legislative Archives National Archives and Records Administrationwww.archives.gov/legislativeHandout

The Declaration of the Rights of Man and of the Citizen, 1789

National Assembly of France

The representatives of the people of France, formed into a National Assembly, considering that ignorance, neglect, or contempt of human rights, are the sole causes of public misfortunes and corruptions of Government, have resolved to set forth in a solemn declaration, these natural, imprescriptible, and inalienable rights: that this declaration being constantly present to the minds of the members of the body social, they may be for ever kept attentive to their rights and their duties; that the acts of the legislative and executive powers of government, being capable of being every moment compared with the end of political institutions, may be more respected; and also, that the future claims of the citizens, being directed by simple and incontestable principles, may tend to the maintenance of the Constitution, and the general happiness. For these reasons, the National Assembly doth recognize and declare, in the presence of the Supreme Being, and with the hope of his blessing and favour, the following sacred rights of men and of citizens:

I. Men are born, and always continue, free and equal in respect of their rights. Civil distinctions, therefore, can be founded only on public utility.

II. The end of all political associations, is the preservation of the natural and imprescriptible rights of man; and these rights are liberty, property, security, and resistance of oppression.

III. The nation is essentially the source of all sovereignty; nor can any individual, or any body of men, be entitled to any authority which is not expressly derived from it.

IV. Political liberty consists in the power of doing whatever does not injure another. The exercise of the natural rights of every man, has no other limits than those which are necessary to secure to every other man the free exercise of the same rights; and these limits are determinable only by the law.

V. The law ought to prohibit only actions hurtful to society. What is not prohibited by the law, should not be hindered; nor should any one be compelled to that which the law does not require.

VI. The law is an expression of the will of the community. All citizens have a right to concur, either personally, or by their representatives, in its formation. It should be the same to all, whether it protects or punishes; and all being equal in its sight, are equally eligible to all honours, places, and employments, according to their different abilities, without any other distinction than that created by their virtues and talents.

VII. No man should be accused, arrested, or held in confinement, except in cases determined by the law, and according to the forms which it has prescribed. All who promote, solicit, execute, or cause to be executed, arbitrary orders, ought to be punished, and every citizen called upon, or apprehended by virtue of the law, ought immediately to obey, and renders himself culpable by resistance.

VIII. The law ought to impose no other penalties but such as are absolutely and evidently necessary; and no one ought to be punished, but in virtue of a law promulgated before the offence, and legally applied.

IX. Every man being presumed innocent till he has been convicted, whenever his detention becomes indispensable, all rigour to him, more than is necessary to secure his person, ought to be provided against by the law.

X. No man ought to be molested on account of his opinions, not even on account of his religious opinions, provided his avowal of them does not disturb the public order established by law.

XI. The unrestrained communication of thoughts and opinions being one of the most precious rights of man, every citizen may speak, write, and publish freely, provided he is responsible for the abuse of this liberty, in cases determined by law.

XII. A public force being necessary to give security to the rights of men and of citizens, that force is instituted for the benefit of the community and not for the particular benefit of the persons to whom it is intrusted.

XIII. A common contribution being necessary for the support of the public force, and for defraying the other expenses of government, it ought to be divided equally among the members of the community, according to their abilities.

XIV. Every citizen has a right, either by himself or his representative, to a free voice in determining the necessity of public contributions, the appropriation of them, and their account, mode of assessment, and duration.

XV. Every community has had a right to demand of all its agents an account of their conduct.

XVI. Every community in which a separation of powers and a security of rights is not provided for, wants a constitution.

XVII. The right to property being inviolable and sacred, no one ought to be deprived of it, except in cases of evident public necessity, legally ascertained, and on condition of a previous just indemnity

<https://constitutionnet.org/sites/default/files/declaration_of_the_rights_of_man_1789.pdf>

THE UNIVERSAL DECLARATION
OF Human Rights

UNITED NATIONS

The Universal Declaration of Human Rights

The Universal Declaration of Human Rights (UDHR) is a milestone document in the history of human rights. Drafted by representatives with different legal and cultural backgrounds from all regions of the world, the Declaration was proclaimed by the United Nations General Assembly in Paris on 10 December 1948 (General Assembly resolution 217 A) as a common standard of achievements for all peoples and all nations. It sets out, for the first time, fundamental human rights to be universally protected and it has been translated into over 500 languages.

Preamble

Whereas recognition of the inherent dignity and of the equal and inalienable rights of all members of the human family is the foundation of freedom, justice and peace in the world,

Whereas disregard and contempt for human rights have resulted in barbarous acts which have outraged the conscience of mankind, and the advent of a world in which human beings shall enjoy freedom of speech and belief and freedom from fear and want has been proclaimed as the highest aspiration of the common people,

Whereas it is essential, if man is not to be compelled to have recourse, as a last resort, to rebellion against tyranny and oppression, that human rights should be protected by the rule of law,

Whereas it is essential to promote the development of friendly relations between nations,

Whereas the peoples of the United Nations have in the Charter reaffirmed their faith in fundamental human rights, in the dignity and worth of the human person and in the equal rights of men and women and have determined to promote social progress and better standards of life in larger freedom,

Whereas Member States have pledged themselves to achieve, in co-operation with the United Nations, the promotion of universal respect for and observance of human rights and fundamental freedoms,

Whereas a common understanding of these rights and freedoms is of the greatest importance for the full realization of this pledge,

Now, Therefore THE GENERAL ASSEMBLY proclaims THIS UNIVERSAL DECLARATION OF HUMAN RIGHTS as a common standard of achievement for all peoples and all nations, to the end that every individual and every organ of society, keeping this Declaration constantly in mind, shall strive by teaching and education to promote respect for these rights and freedoms and by progressive measures, national and international, to secure their universal and effective recognition and observance, both among the peoples of Member States themselves and among the peoples of territories under their jurisdiction. All human beings are born free and equal in dignity and rights. They are endowed with reason and conscience and should act towards one another in a spirit of brotherhood.

Article 1.

Everyone has the right to life, liberty and security of person.

Article 2.

Everyone is entitled to all the rights and freedoms set forth in this Declaration, without distinction of any kind, such as race, colour, sex, language, religion, political or other opinion, national or social origin, property, birth or other status. Furthermore, no distinction shall be made on the basis of the political, jurisdictional or international status of the country or territory to which a person belongs, whether it be independent, trust, non-self-governing or under any other limitation of sovereignty.

Article 3.

Everyone has the right to life, liberty and security of person.

Article 4.

No one shall be held in slavery or servitude; slavery and the slave trade shall be prohibited in all their forms.

Article 5.

No one shall be subjected to torture or to cruel, inhuman or degrading treatment or punishment.

Article 6.

Everyone has the right to recognition everywhere as a person before the law.

Article 7.

All are equal before the law and are entitled without any discrimination to equal protection of the law. All are entitled to equal protection against any discrimination in violation of this Declaration and against any incitement to such discrimination.

Article 8.

Everyone has the right to an effective remedy by the competent national tribunals for acts violating the fundamental rights granted him by the constitution or by law.

Article 9.

No one shall be subjected to arbitrary arrest, detention or exile.

Article 10.

Everyone is entitled in full equality to a fair and public hearing by an independent and impartial tribunal, in the determination of his rights and obligations and of any criminal charge against him.

Article 11.

(1) Everyone charged with a penal offence has the right to be presumed innocent until proved guilty according to law in a public trial at which he has had all the guarantees necessary for his defence.

(2) No one shall be held guilty of any penal offence on account of any act or omission which did not constitute a penal offence, under national or international law, at the time when it was committed. Nor shall a heavier penalty be imposed than the one that was applicable at the time the penal offence was committed.

Article 12.

No one shall be subjected to arbitrary interference with his privacy, family, home or correspondence, nor to attacks upon his honour and reputation. Everyone has the right to the protection of the law against such interference or attacks.

Article 13.

(1) Everyone has the right to freedom of movement and residence within the borders of each state.

(2) Everyone has the right to leave any country, including his own, and to return to his country.

Article 14.

(1) Everyone has the right to seek and to enjoy in other countries asylum from persecution.
(2) This right may not be invoked in the case of prosecutions genuinely arising from non-political crimes or from acts contrary to the purposes and principles of the United Nations.

Article 15.

(1) Everyone has the right to a nationality.
(2) No one shall be arbitrarily deprived of his nationality nor denied the right to change his nationality.

Article 16.

(1) Men and women of full age, without any limitation due to race, nationality or religion, have the right to marry and to found a family. They are entitled to equal rights as to marriage, during marriage and at its dissolution.
(2) Marriage shall be entered into only with the free and full consent of the intending spouses.
(3) The family is the natural and fundamental group unit of society and is entitled to protection by society and the State.

Article 17.

(1) Everyone has the right to own property alone as well as in association with others.
(2) No one shall be arbitrarily deprived of his property.

Article 18.

Everyone has the right to freedom of thought, conscience and religion; this right includes freedom to change his religion or belief, and freedom, either alone or in community with others and in public or private, to manifest his religion or belief in teaching, practice, worship and observance.

Article 19.

Everyone has the right to freedom of opinion and expression; this right includes freedom to hold opinions without interference and to seek, receive and impart information and ideas through any media and regardless of frontiers.

Article 20.

(1) Everyone has the right to freedom of peaceful assembly and association.
(2) No one may be compelled to belong to an association.

Article 21.

(1) Everyone has the right to take part in the government of his country, directly or through freely chosen representatives.
(2) Everyone has the right of equal access to public service in his country.
(3) The will of the people shall be the basis of the authority of government; this will shall be expressed in periodic and genuine elections which shall be by universal and equal suffrage and shall be held by secret vote or by equivalent free voting procedures.

Article 22.

Everyone, as a member of society, has the right to social security and is entitled to realization, through national effort and international co-operation and in accordance with the organization and resources of each State, of the economic, social and cultural rights indispensable for his dignity and the free development of his personality.

Article 23.

(1) Everyone has the right to work, to free choice of employment, to just and favourable conditions of work and to protection against unemployment.
(2) Everyone, without any discrimination, has the right to equal pay for equal work.
(3) Everyone who works has the right to just and favourable remuneration ensuring for himself and his family an existence worthy of human dignity, and supplemented, if necessary, by other means of social protection.
(4) Everyone has the right to form and to join trade unions for the protection of his interests.

Article 24.

Everyone has the right to rest and leisure, including reasonable limitation of working hours and periodic holidays with pay.

Article 25.

(1) Everyone has the right to a standard of living adequate for the health and well-being of himself and of his family, including food, clothing, housing and medical care and necessary social services, and the right to security in the event of unemployment, sickness, disability, widowhood, old age or other lack of livelihood in circumstances beyond his control.
(2) Motherhood and childhood are entitled to special care and assistance. All children, whether born in or out of wedlock, shall enjoy the same social protection.

Article 26.

(1) Everyone has the right to education. Education shall be free, at least in the elementary and fundamental stages. Elementary education shall be compulsory. Technical and professional

education shall be made generally available and higher education shall be equally accessible to all on the basis of merit.

(2) Education shall be directed to the full development of the human personality and to the strengthening of respect for human rights and fundamental freedoms. It shall promote understanding, tolerance and friendship among all nations, racial or religious groups, and shall further the activities of the United Nations for the maintenance of peace.

(3) Parents have a prior right to choose the kind of education that shall be given to their children.

Article 27.

(1) Everyone has the right freely to participate in the cultural life of the community, to enjoy the arts and to share in scientific advancement and its benefits.

(2) Everyone has the right to the protection of the moral and material interests resulting from any scientific, literary or artistic production of which he is the author.

Article 28.

Everyone is entitled to a social and international order in which the rights and freedoms set forth in this Declaration can be fully realized.

Article 29.

(1) Everyone has duties to the community in which alone the free and full development of his personality is possible.

(2) In the exercise of his rights and freedoms, everyone shall be subject only to such limitations as are determined by law solely for the purpose of securing due recognition and respect for the rights and freedoms of others and of meeting the just requirements of morality, public order and the general welfare in a democratic society.

(3) These rights and freedoms may in no case be exercised contrary to the purposes and principles of the United Nations.

Article 30.

Nothing in this Declaration may be interpreted as implying for any State, group or person any right to engage in any activity or to perform any act aimed at the destruction of any of the rights and freedoms set forth herein.

<https://www.un.org/en/universal-declaration-human-rights/>

See also, United Nations Declaration on the Rights of Indigenous Peoples:

<https://www.un.org/development/desa/indigenouspeoples/wp-content/uploads/sites/19/2018/11/UNDRIP_E_web.pdf>

References

In order of mention within chapters.

Chapter 1: Thinking about democracy: tools for understanding

Drew DeSilver, "Despite Global Concerns about Democracy, More than Half of Countries are Democratic," Fact Tank, Pew Research Center, May 14, 2019, <https://www.pewresearch.org/fact-tank/2019/05/14/more-than-half-of-countries-are-democratic/>.

Bernard Crick, *Democracy: A Very Short Introduction*, Oxford: Oxford University Press, 2002.

Tom Christiano and Sameer Bajaj, "Democracy," *The Stanford Encyclopedia of Philosophy* (Fall 2021 Edition), Edward N. Zalta (ed.), <https://plato.stanford.edu/archives/fall2021/entries/democracy/>.

Mark J. Rozell and Clyde Wilcox, *Federalism: A Very Short Introduction*, New York: Oxford University Press, 2019, pp. 92–7.

Brennan Center for Justice, "Voting Laws Roundup: February 2022," February 9, 2022, <https://www.brennancenter.org/our-work/research-reports/voting-laws-roundup-february-2022>.

Walter Bagehot, *The English Constitution*, 1873, History of Economic Thought, 2nd ed., p. 13, <https://historyofeconomicthought.mcmaster.ca/bagehot/constitution.pdf>.

Amartya Sen, "Democracy and Its Global Roots," *The New Republic*, October 4, 2003, pp. 28–35.

Jacques Rancière, *Hatred of Democracy*, trans. Steve Corcoran, London: Verso, 2007.

Chapter 2: Democracy in the ancient world: Greece, Rome, and beyond

Sviatoslav Dmitriev, *The Birth of the Athenian Community, From Solon to Cleisthenes*, London: Routledge, 2017.

Martin Bernal, *Black Athena: Afroasiatic Roots of Classical Civilization*, Volume II: *The Archaeological and Documentary Evidence*, New Brunswick, NJ: Rutgers University Press, 1991.

Moses Hadas, "The Social Revolution in Third-Century Sparta," *Source: The Classical Weekly* 26, no. 9 (December 12, 1932): 65–8.

H. G. Frederickson, "Confucius and the Moral Basis of Bureaucracy," *Administration & Society* 33, no. 6 (2002): 610–28. doi:10.1177/0095399702336002

R. S. Sharma, *Aspects of Political Ideas and Institutions in Ancient India*, 3rd ed. Motilal Banarsidass, 1991.

Stephen Stockwell, "Before Athens: Early Popular Government in Phoenicia and Greek City-States," in Benjamin Isakhan and Stephen Stockwell, eds., *The Secret History of Democracy*, London: Palgrave Macmillan, 2011, pp. 35–48.

Plato, *Euthyphro*, trans. Benjamin Jowett, Project Gutenberg, 2008 <https://www.gutenberg.org/files/1642/1642-h/1642-h.htm> sec. 15, e 4.

Plato, *The Republic*, trans. Benjamin Jowett, Project Gutenberg, 2017, <https://www.gutenberg.org/files/55201/55201-h/55201-h.htm>, Book 3, 410a and Book 7, 540, b–c.

Aristotle, *Nicomachean Ethics*, trans. W. D. Ross, The Internet Classics Archives, <http://classics.mit.edu/Aristotle/nicomachaen.html>; *Politics*, trans. Benjamin Jowett, The Internet Classics Archives, Book 6, ch. 2 and Book 7, ch. 2, 1253 a, 1–5.

Cicero, *On Obligations: De Officiis*, trans. P. G. Walsh, Oxford World's Classics, Reissue Edition, 2008, 20, 53; *De Re Publica (On the Republic)*, 1, 37, 38, 34; *De Legibus (On the Laws)*, Loeb Classical Library No. 213, trans. Clinton W. Keyes, 1928/2000, I, 15.

Chapter 3: Democracy in the medieval and Renaissance world

Magna Carta, Middle Ages and Renaissance, and specific locales in Seymour Martin Lipset, editor-in-chief, *The Encyclopedia of Democracy*, Washington, DC: Congressional Quarterly Inc., 1995, 4 vols.

David Schmidtz and Jason Brennan, *A Brief History of Liberty*, Malden, MA: Wiley-Blackwell, 2010.

John Kilcullen and Jonathan Robinson, "Medieval Political Philosophy," *The Stanford Encyclopedia of Philosophy* (Winter 2019 Edition), Edward N. Zalta (ed.), <https://plato.stanford.edu/archives/win2019/entries/medieval-political/>.

John P. McCormick, "Addressing the Political Exception: Machiavelli's 'Accidents' and the Mixed Regime," *The American Political Science Review* 87, no. 4 (1993): 888–900. Accessed January 24, 2021. doi:10.2307/2938821.

UNESCO, "Manden Charter, Proclaimed in Kurukan Fuga," Intangible Cultural Heritage, 2009. <https://ich.unesco.org/en/RL/manden-charter-proclaimed-in-kurukan-fuga-00290>.

Lizzie Wade, "It Wasn't just Greece: Archaeologists Find Early Democratic Societies in the Americas," *Science Magazine*, March 15, 2017, <https://www.sciencemag.org/news/2017/03/it-wasnt-just-greece-archaeologists-find-early-democratic-societies-americas doi:10.1126/science.aal0905)>

M. Abdalla and H. Rane, "Behind a Veil: Islam's Democratic History," *Semantic Scholar*, 2011, <https://www.semanticscholar.org/paper/Behind-a-Veil%3A-Islam%E2%80%99s-Democratic-History-Abdalla-Rane/4e7afc73a0062132c54894e79156f92556e93883>.

Jørgen Møller, "The Medieval Roots of Democracy," *Journal of Democracy* 26 no. 3 (2015): 110–23. *Project MUSE*, doi:10.1353/jod.2015.0042.

Chapter 4: The social contract: consent of those governed

Peter Ackroyd, *Rebellion: The History of England from James I to the Glorious Revolution*, New York: St. Martin's Press, 2014.

Thomas Hobbes, *Leviathan*, ed. Edwin Curley (with introduction and biographical material), Indianapolis: Hackett, 2014, ch. XIII, ch. XXVI, 9, 13, ch. XVII, 7.

John Locke, *Second Treatise of Government*, in *Two Treatises of Government*, ed. W. S. Carpenter, Guernsey Press, 1924/1989, chs. V and XVIII.

John Locke, *The Social Contract and Other Later Political Writings*, ed. and trans. Victor Gourevitch, Cambridge: Cambridge University Press, 1997, ch. II, 6, ch. V, 28, ch. XIX, 222.

Robert Nozick, *Anarchy, State, and Utopia*, New York: Basic Books, 1974, pp. 174–5.

Jean-Jacques Rousseau, *The Social Contract and the First and Second Discourses*, ed. Susan Dunn, New Haven: Yale University Press, 2002.

Arthur M. Melzer, *The Natural Goodness of Man: On the System of Rousseau's Thought*, Chicago: University of Chicago Press, 1990.

Chapter 5: Rights and revolutions: (exclusive) political equality

The Confessions of J. J. Rousseau, produced by David Widger, Gutenberg Files, <https://www.gutenberg.org/files/3913/3913-h/3913-h.htm>, p. 357.

US Library of Congress, "American Revolution: Resource Guide," <https://guides.loc.gov/american-revolution>.

Gordon S. Wood, *The American Revolution: A History*, New York: Modern Library, 2002.

Friedrich Gentz, *The Origin and Principles of the American Revolution, Compared with the Origin and Principles of the French Revolution*, ed. Peter Koslowski, trans. John Quincy Adams, Asbury Dinkins: 1800/Indianapolis: Liberty Fund, 2012.

Jeremy D. Popkin, *A Short History of the French Revolution*, New York: Routledge, 7th ed. 2020.

Edmund Burke, *Reflections on the Revolution in France*, Anodos Books, UK, 2019; Project Gutenberg, p. 15.

Jean-Jacques Rousseau, *Reveries of the Solitary Walker*, V. ed. Colin Choat, 2022, <https://gutenberg.net.au/ebooks19/1900981h.html>.

David Hackett Fischer, *Albion's Seed: Four British Folkways in America*, New York: Oxford University Press, 1989.

Chapter 6: Social progressivism: toward democracy in society

Eric A. Shelman and Stephen Lazorwitz, *Out of the Darkness: The Story of Mary Ellen Wilson*, Dolphin Moon, 1999.

Margaret Meek Lange, "Progress," *The Stanford Encyclopedia of Philosophy*, Edward N. Zalta, ed., Winter 2019, <https://plato.stanford.edu/archives/win2019/entries/progress/>.

Jeremy Bentham, *An Introduction to the Principles of Morals and Legislation*, <https://www.earlymoderntexts.com/assets/pdfs/bentham1780.pdf>.

John Stuart Mill, *The Collected Works of John Stuart Mill*, ed. J. M. Robson, 33 vols., Toronto: University of Toronto Press,

London: Routledge and Kegan Paul, 1963–91, available at Liberty
Fund, <https://oll.libertyfund.org/title/robson-collected-works-
of-john-stuart-mill-in-33-vols>.

Mary Wollstonecraft, *Vindication of the Rights of Woman*, Enhanced
Media, 1792/2014.

Karl Marx and Friedrich Engels, *Collected Works*, New York and
London: International Publishers, 1975.

Renée Jacobs, "The Iroquois Great Law of Peace and the United States
Constitution: How the Founding Fathers Ignored the Clan
Mothers," *Am. Indian L. Rev.* 16, no. 497 (1991), <https://
digitalcommons.law.ou.edu/ailr/vol16/iss2/5>.

Chapter 7: New democracies and new conceptions of democracy

Hannah Arendt, *Between Past and Future*, New York: Viking Press,
1961, pp. 234–5.

John Rawls, *A Theory of Justice*, Chicago: University of Chicago
Press, 1971.

Amartya Sen, "Equality of What?," in Sterling M. McMurrin, ed.,
Tanner Lectures on Human Values, Cambridge: Cambridge
University Press, 1979, pp. 197–220.

Mohandas Karamchand Gandhi, *The Essential Writings of
Mahatma Gandhi*, ed. Raghavan Iyer, Delhi: Oxford University
Press, 1991.

Ashutosh Varshney, "The Self-Correcting Mechanisms of Indian
Democracy," *Seminar*, Delhi, January 1995.

Juan Williams, *Eyes on the Prize: America's Civil Rights Movement,
1954–1965*, New York: Penguin, 1987/2013.

Leonard Thompson and Lynn Berat, *A History of South Africa*, New
Haven: Yale University Press, 2012.

Chapter 8: The future of democracy: threats and resilience

Thomas G. Weiss, "The United Nations: Before, during and after
1945," *International Affairs* 91, no. 6 (November 2015): 1221–35,
DOI: 10.1111/1468-2346.12450 <https://www.researchgate.net/
publication/284102686_The_United_Nations_Before_during_
and_after_1945>.

Steven Levitsky and Daniel Ziblatt, *How Democracies Die*, New York:
Crown Publishing, 2018.

Isaiah Berlin, "Two Concepts of Liberty," 1958 Inaugural lecture as Chichele Professor of Social and Political Theory at Oxford University, in Isaiah Berlin, *Four Essays on Liberty*, Oxford: Oxford University Press, 1969. Accessed from <https://www.aspeninstitute.org/wp-content/uploads/files/content/docs/BERLIN_TWO_CONCEPTS_OF_LIBERTY_(AS08).PDF>.

United Nations, "Universal Declaration of Human Rights," <https://www.un.org/en/about-us/universal-declaration-of-human-rights>.

Arthur F. Bentley, *The Process of Government*, Chicago: University of Chicago Press, 1908.

W. E. B. Du Bois, *The Philadelphia Negro: A Social Study*, Elijah Anderson, Introduction, Philadelphia: University of Pennsylvania Press, 1899/1996.

United Nations, "What is Human Security," Trust Fund for Human Security, <https://www.un.org/humansecurity/what-is-human-security/>.

Brian L. Keeley, "Of Conspiracy Theories," *Journal of Philosophy* 96, no. 3 (March 1999): 109–26. <https://www.jstor.org/stable/2564659?seq=1>.

Mark Fenster, *Conspiracy Theories: Secrecy and Power in American Culture*, Minneapolis: University of Minnesota Press, 1999/2008.

John Stuart Mill, *On Liberty*, Excerpts, <openmindplatform.org>, p. 22, full text Project Gutenberg, 2011.

Karl Popper, "Karl Popper on Democracy," From the archives: the open society and its enemies revisited, *The Economist*, April 23, 1988/January 31, 2016, <https://www.economist.com/democracy-in-america/2016/01/31/from-the-archives-the-open-society-and-its-enemies-revisited>.

Ted Piccone, "COVID-19 has Worsened a Shaky Rule of Law Environment," Brookings, April 15, 2021 <https://www.brookings.edu/blog/order-from-chaos/2021/04/20/covid-19-has-worsened-a-shaky-rule-of-law-environment/?utm_campaign=brookings->.

Further reading

Chapter 1: Thinking about democracy: tools for understanding

Noam Chomsky, *Occupy*, London: Zuccotti Press/Penguin Press, 2012.

Kimberle Crenshaw, "Demarginalizing the Intersection of Race and Sex: A Black Feminist Critique of Antidiscrimination Doctrine, Feminist Theory and Antiracist Politics," University of Chicago Legal Forum: Vol. 1989: Iss. 1, Article 8. Available at: <http://chicagounbound.uchicago.edu/uclf/vol1989/iss1/8>.

José L. Falguera, Concha Martínez-Vidal, and Gideon Rosen, "Abstract Objects," *The Stanford Encyclopedia of Philosophy* (Summer 2022 Edition), Edward N. Zalta (ed.), forthcoming <https://plato.stanford.edu/archives/sum2022/entries/abstract-objects/> and Dennis Earl, "The Classical Theory of Concepts," *Internet Encyclopedia of Philosophy*, <https://iep.utm.edu/classical-theory-of-concepts/>.

Rob Garver, "One Year After the Capitol Riot, Many Americans See US Democracy in Peril," *VOA* January 5, 2022 1:11 PM, USA.

Alan Hattersley, *A Short History of Democracy*, Cambridge: Cambridge University Press, 1930.

Naomi Zack, *Applicative Justice: A Pragmatic Empirical Approach to Racial Injustice*, London: Rowman & Littlefield, 2016.

Chapter 2: Democracy in the ancient world: Greece, Rome, and beyond

Keith R. Bradley, *Slavery and Rebellion in the Roman World, 140 B.C.–70 B.C.* Bloomington, IN: Indiana University Press, 1989, ch. V, "The Slave War of Spartacus," pp. 83–101.

Anthony Everitt, *Cicero: The Life and Times of Rome's Greatest Politician*, New York: Random House, 2001.

Cynthia Farrar, *The Origins of Democratic Thinking: The Invention of Politics in Classical Athens*, Cambridge: Cambridge University Press, 1988.

Thomas R. Marin, *Ancient Rome: From Romulus to Justinian*, New Haven: Yale University Press, 2012.

E. W. Robinson, *The First Democracies*, Berlin: Franz Steiner Verlag, 1997.

Chapter 3: Democracy in the medieval and Renaissance world

Anthony Black, *Political Thought in Europe, 1250-1450*, Cambridge: Cambridge University Press, 1992.

Joseph Henrich, *The Weirdest People in the World: How the West Became Psychologically Peculiar and Particularly Prosperous*, New York: Farrar, Straus, Giroux, 2020.

Paul B. Newman, *Daily Life in the Middle Ages*, Jefferson, NC: McFarland and Co., 2001.

TimeMaps, "Medieval Europe: Government, Politics and War," <https://www.timemaps.com/encyclopedia/medieval-europe-government-warfare/>.

Chapter 4: The social contract: consent of those governed

M. J. Montero Burgos, H. Sanchiz Álvarez de Toledo, R. A. González Lezcano, and A. Galán de Mera. "The Sedentary Process and the Evolution of Energy Consumption in Eight Native American Dwellings: Analyzing Sustainability in Traditional Architecture," *Sustainability* 12, no. 5 (2020): 1810. <https://doi.org/10.3390/su12051810>.

Eleanor Curran, "Can Rights Curb the Hobbesian Sovereign? The Full Right to Self-Preservation, Duties of Sovereignty and the

Limitations of Hohfeld," *Law and Philosophy* 25, no. 2 (2006): 243–65. <http://www.jstor.org/stable/27639430>.

Robert Darnton, *The Great Cat Massacre and Other Episodes in French Cultural History*, New York: Perseus Group, 1984/2009, ch. 6, "Readers Respond to Rousseau: The Fabrication of Romantic Sensitivity."

David Edmonds and John Eidinow, *Rousseau's Dog: Two Great Thinkers at War in the Age of Enlightenment*, New York: Harper Collins, 2006.

Rachel Foxley, *The Levellers: Radical Political Thought in the English Revolution*, Manchester: Manchester University Press, 2013.

Otto Friedrich von Gierke and Ernst Troeltsch, *Natural Law and the Theory of Society 1500 to 1800*, trans. Sir Ernest Barker, Cambridge: Cambridge University Press, 1950.

Thomas Hobbes, *De Cive*, ed. Howard Warrender, Oxford: Clarendon Press, 1983.

C. B. Macpherson, *The Political Theory of Possessive Individualism*, Oxford: Oxford University Press, 1962.

Jean Jacques Rousseau, *The Reveries of the Solitary Walker*, ed. Colin Choat, Project Gutenberg of Australia eBook, 2019, eBook No.: 1900981h.html <http://gutenberg.net.au/ebooks19/1900981h.html>.

George S. Snyderman, "The Functions of Wampum," *Proceedings of the American Philosophical Society* 98, no. 6 (1954): 469–94. JSTOR, <http://www.jstor.org/stable/3143870>. Accessed June 12, 2022.

Chapter 5: Rights and revolutions: (exclusive) political equality

Philip B. Kurland and Ralph Lerner, eds., *The Founders' Constitution*, Chicago: University of Chicago Press, 1987, <http://press-pubs.uchicago.edu/founders/>.

Jeremy D. Popkin, *A New World Begins: The History of the French Revolution*, New York: Basic Books, 2019.

Ray Raphael, *A People's History of the American Revolution: How Common People Shaped the Fight for Independence*, New York: New Press, 2016.

Alexis de Tocqueville, *Democracy in America*, Chicago: University of Chicago Press, 2000.

Chapter 6: Social progressivism: toward democracy in society

Jeremy Bentham, "Offences Against One's Self: Paederasty," Columbia University <http://www.columbia.edu/cu/lweb/eresources/exhibitions/sw25/bentham/bentham_offences_1785.pdf>.

Donald N. Duquette, "Child Protection Legal Process: Comparing the United States and Great Britain," *U. Pitt. L. Rev.* 54 (1992): 239.

Eleanor Flexner and Ellen Fitzpatrick, *Century of Struggle: The Woman's Rights Movement in the United States*, 3rd ed., New York: Belknap Press, 1996.

Immanuel Kant, *Idea for a Universal History from a Cosmopolitan Point of View* (1784). Translation by Lewis White Beck. From Immanuel Kant, "On History," The Bobbs-Merrill Co., 1963. <https://www.marxists.org/reference/subject/ethics/kant/universal-history.htm>.

Erica G. Polakoff, "Globalization and Child Labor, Review of the Issues," Journal of Developing Societies 23, nos. 1–2 (2007): 259–83, <https://journals.sagepub.com/doi/pdf/10.1177/016979 6X0602300215?casa_token=CAxys8oxRdYAAAAA%3AI7eu-yG7oMpGFVkA1JGPu3RX6DH9Z2CebyrI07cfg8YTjsTHOOd-nHww57ozsSMIidooY7JfcDAiB&>.

Chris Shore, "Jeremy Bentham's Body Gets A Contentious New Box At UCL," <https://londonist.com/london/jeremy-bentham-s-body-gets-a-new-box>.

Manisha Sinha, *The Slave's Cause: A History of Abolition*, New Haven: Yale University Press, 2016.

Chapter 7: New democracies and new conceptions of democracy

Camille Zubrinsky Charles, "The Dynamics of Racial Residential Segregation," *Annual Review of Sociology* 29, no. 1 (2003): 167–207, <https://www.annualreviews.org/doi/abs/10.1146/annurev.soc.29.010202.100002>.

The Economist, Briefing, "India's Diminishing Democracy—Narendra Modi Threatens to Turn India into a One-Party State," November 28, 2020, <https://www.economist.com/briefing/2020/11/28/narendra-modi-threatens-to-turn-india-into-a-one-party-state#>.

Marika Sherwood, "Colonies, Colonials and World War Two," *BBC News. BBC* 30 (2011). <https://wiki.phalkefactory.net/images/4/4a/Colonies,_Colonials_and_World_War_Two.pdf>.

Naomi Zack, *Progressive Anonymity: From Identity Politics to Evidence-Based Government*, Lanham, MD: Rowman and Littlefield, 2020.

Chapter 8: The future of democracy: threats and resilience

Paulo Friere, *Pedagogy of the Oppressed*, trans. Myra Bergman Ramos, New York: Bloomsbury, 1970.

Jan De Houwer and Dirk Hermans, eds., *Cognition & Emotions: Reviews of Current Research and Theories*, Psychology Press, 2010.

Tana Johnson, "Polarization, Populism, and the Performance of International Organizations During the Coronavirus Crisis," Brookings, December 17, 2020 <https://www.brookings.edu/blog/future-development/2020/12/17/polarization-populism-and-the-performance-of-international-organizations-during-the-coronavirus-crisis/>.

Charles Mackay, *Extraordinary Popular Delusions and the Madness of Crowds*, Richard Bentley, 1841/CreateSpace Independent Publishing Platform; Reprint edition (July 23, 2011).

Condoleezza Rice, Democracy: Stories from the Long Road to Freedom, New York: Hachette Book Group, 2017.

M. N. S. Sellers, *Law, Reason, and Emotion*, Cambridge: Cambridge University Press, 2017.

United Nations, "Declaration on the Rights of Indigenous Peoples," Department of Economic and Social Affairs, Indigenous People, <https://www.un.org/development/desa/indigenouspeoples/declaration-on-the-rights-of-indigenous-peoples.html>.

Naomi Zack, *The American Tragedy of COVID-19: Social and Political Crises of 2020*, London: Rowman & Littlefield, 2020.

Index

For the benefit of digital users, indexed terms that span two pages
(e.g., 52–53) may, on occasion, appear on only one of those pages.

M

Machiavelli, Niccolò di
  Bernardo dei 42
Macron, President Emmanuel 2
Magna Carta (1215) 35, 71
Mali Empire 38
Mandela, Nelson 109–10
Manden Charter (1236) 38
Marshall Plan 100
Marsilius of Padua 40–1
Marx, Karl 82, 87–91
Mary II, Queen of Great Britain
  and Ireland 53
materialism 46, 49–50
measurements of democracy 3
medieval period *see* Middle Ages
Mesopotamia 20–1
Mexico, during the Middle
  Ages 38–9
Middle Ages 33–42
Middle East 20–1
Mill, John Stuart 82, 84–7,
  94–5, 123
Modi, Narendra 114
Møller, Jørge 43
monarchies 33–4, 40–1
  rule of law 35
  threat to private property 57
Montesquieu, Charles-Louis de
  Secondat, Baron de 12–13
morality 6, 9, 28–9
  in arts and sciences 57–8
  within a democratic society 77–9
  effect of human relations 58–60
  political 95–6
Mormon Church 91–2
multiculturalism 20
Mussolini, Benito 99–100

N

Nabhaga 23
National Woman Suffrage
  Association (NWSA) 92–3

nation states 10
nativism 76
natural disasters 115–16
natural law 41
natural rights 50–4, 56–7
  critiques 82–3
  and equality 62–3
  and morality 58–60
Nehru, Jawaharlal 106–7
neoliberalism 81
Nicholas of Cusa 40–1
nonideal theory 104
normative approaches 8–9
Norway 36
Nozick, Robert 55

O

Occupy Movement 7–8
Ockham, William of 41
Otto I the Great, Holy Roman
  Emperor 38

P

Parks, Rosa 107
peace, as sign of progress 81–2
Peisistratus 26–7
Peloponnesian War 27
penal system 83
Pence, Mike 1–2
Pericles 27
Pew Research Center 3
Philip IV the Fair, King of
  France 37
Phoenicia 20–2
Plato 20, 22, 25, 28–9
political morality 95–6
political participation 10–11
  debates about 11–12
  as a virtue 30
political progressivism 79–80
Polybius 21–2
Popper, Karl 101–3, 111, 124–5
populism 11–12, 124

Democracy

CITIZENSHIP
A Very Short Introduction
Richard Bellamy

Interest in citizenship has never been higher. But what does it mean to be a citizen of a modern, complex community? Why is citizenship important? Can we create citizenship, and can we test for it? In this fascinating Very Short Introduction, Richard Bellamy explores the answers to these questions and more in a clear and accessible way. He approaches the subject from a political perspective, to address the complexities behind the major topical issues. Discussing the main models of citizenship, exploring how ideas of citizenship have changed through time from ancient Greece to the present, and examining notions of rights and democracy, he reveals the irreducibly political nature of citizenship today.

> 'Citizenship is a vast subject for a short introduction, but Richard Bellamy has risen to the challenge with aplomb.'
>
> Mark Garnett, TLS

www.oup.com/vsi

TOCQUEVILLE
A Very Short Introduction
Harvey Mansfield

No one has ever described American democracy with more accurate insight or more profoundly than Alexis de Tocqueville. After meeting with Americans on extensive travels in the United States, and intense study of documents and authorities, he authored the landmark *Democracy in America*, publishing its two volumes in 1835 and 1840. Ever since, this book has been the best source for every serious attempt to understand America and democracy itself. Yet Tocqueville himself remains a mystery behind the elegance of his style. In this *Very Short Introduction*, Harvey Mansfield addresses his subject as a thinker, clearly and incisively exploring Tocqueville's writings-not only his masterpiece, but also his secret *Recollections*, intended for posterity alone, and his unfinished work on his native France, *The Old Regime and the Revolution*.

www.oup.com/vsi

AMERICAN POLITICAL PARTIES AND ELECTIONS
A Very Short Introduction
Sandy L. Maisel

Few Americans and even fewer citizens of other nations understand the electoral process in the United States. Still fewer understand the role played by political parties in the electoral process or the ironies within the system. Participation in elections in the United States is much lower than in the vast majority of mature democracies. Perhaps this is because of the lack of competition in a country where only two parties have a true chance of winning, despite the fact that a large number of citizens claim allegiance to neither and think badly of both. Studying these factors, you begin to get a very clear picture indeed of the problems that underlay this much trumpeted electoral system.

www.oup.com/vsi

FREE SPEECH
A Very Short Introduction
Nigel Warburton

'I disapprove of what you say, but I will defend to the death your right to say it' This slogan, attributed to Voltaire, is frequently quoted by defenders of free speech. Yet it is rare to find anyone prepared to defend all expression in every circumstance, especially if the views expressed incite violence. So where do the limits lie? What is the real value of free speech? Here, Nigel Warburton offers a concise guide to important questions facing modern society about the value and limits of free speech: Where should a civilized society draw the line? Should we be free to offend other people's religion? Are there good grounds for censoring pornography? Has the Internet changed everything? This Very Short Introduction is a thought-provoking, accessible, and up-to-date examination of the liberal assumption that free speech is worth preserving at any cost.

'The genius of Nigel Warburton's *Free Speech* lies not only in its extraordinary clarity and incisiveness. Just as important is the way Warburton addresses freedom of speech - and attempts to stifle it - as an issue for the 21st century. More than ever, we need this book.'

Denis Dutton, University of Canterbury, New Zealand

HUMAN RIGHTS
A Very Short Introduction
Andrew Clapham

An appeal to human rights in the face of injustice can be a heartfelt and morally justified demand for some, while for others it remains merely an empty slogan. Taking an international perspective and focusing on highly topical issues such as torture, arbitrary detention, privacy, health and discrimination, this *Very Short Introduction* will help readers to understand for themselves the controversies and complexities behind this vitally relevant issue. Looking at the philosophical justification for rights, the historical origins of human rights and how they are formed in law, Andrew Clapham explains what our human rights actually are, what they might be, and where the human rights movement is heading.

www.oup.com/vsi

THE AMERICAN PRESIDENCY
A Very Short Introduction
Charles O. Jones

This marvellously concise survey is packed with information about the presidency, some of it quite surprising. We learn, for example, that the Founders adopted the word "president" over "governor" and other alternatives because it suggested a light hand, as in one who presides, rather than rules. Indeed, the Constitutional Convention first agreed to a weak chief executive elected by congress for one seven-year term, later calling for independent election and separation of powers. Jones sheds much light on how assertive leaders, such as Andrew Jackson, Theodore Roosevelt, and FDR enhanced the power of the presidency, and illuminating how such factors as philosophy (Reagan's anti-Communist conservatism), the legacy of previous presidencies (Jimmy Carter following Watergate), relations with Congress, and the impact of outside events have all influenced presidential authority.

> "In this brief but timely book, a leading expert takes us back to the creation of the presidency and insightfully explains the challenges of executive leadership in a separated powers system."
>
> George C. Edwards III, Distinguished Professor of Political Science, Texas A&M University

www.oup.com/vsi